Contents

Turner to Tate: A Short History

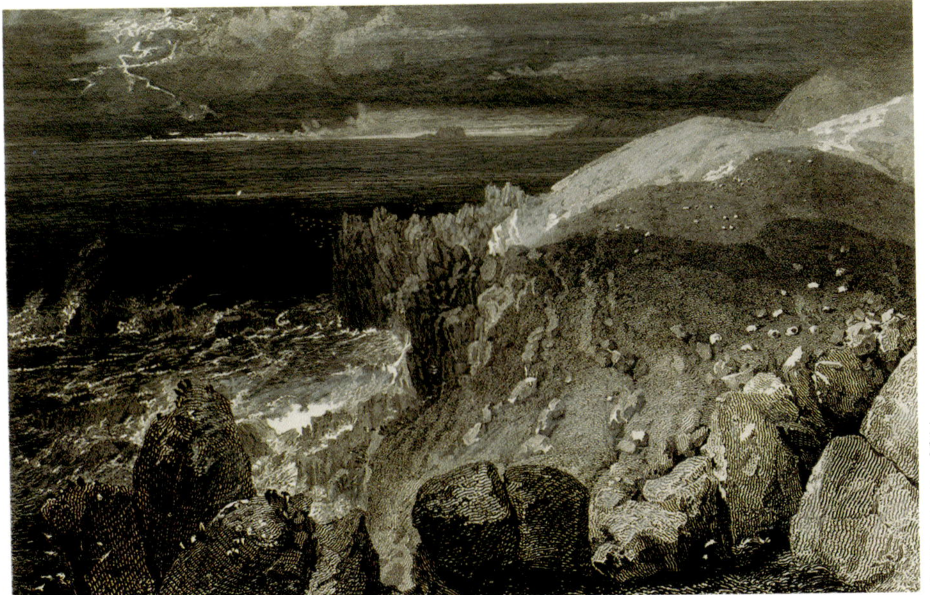

© Tate, London 2011

J.M.W. Turner, Land's End, Cornwall, *from* Picturesque Views on the Southern Coast of England, *1818. Intaglio print on paper, 14.2 x 22.1 cm*

In the summer of 1811 the artist J.M.W. Turner set off on a tour of the West Country that eventually took him all the way down to Land's End. Today around 5 million people visit Cornwall each year, but in the 1800s hardly anyone made this journey in search of pleasure or leisure – still less for anything to do with art. Just getting from London to

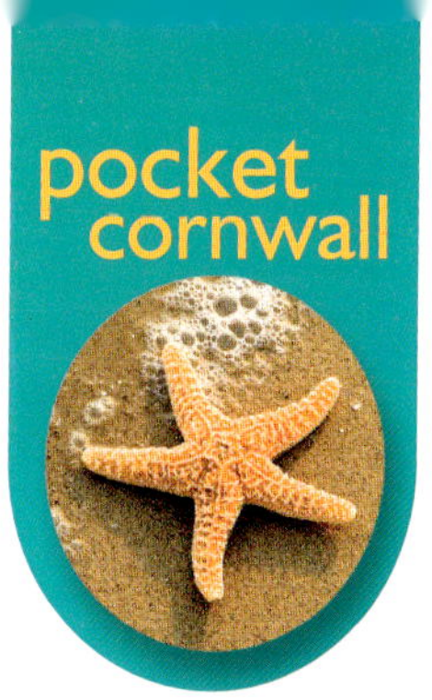

Art in Cornwall

Michael Bird

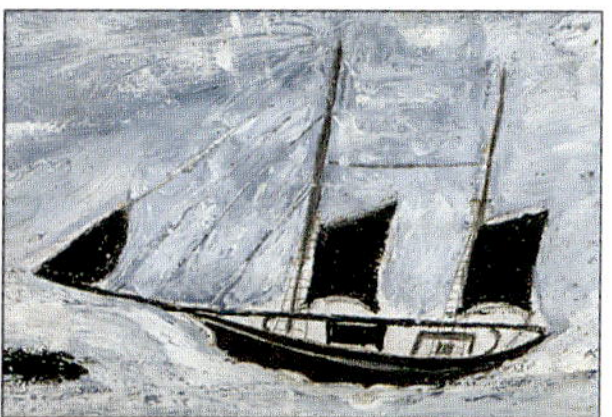

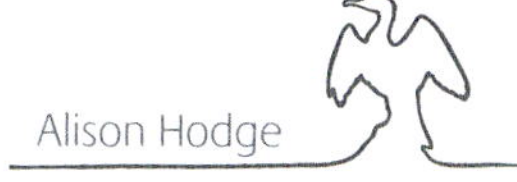

For my mother and father

First published in 2012 by
Alison Hodge, 2 Clarence Place,
Penzance, Cornwall TR18 2QA
info@alison-hodge.co.uk
www.alisonhodgepublishers.co.uk

ISBN-13 978-0-906720-75-2

British Library Cataloguing-in-Publication Data
A catalogue record for this book is available from the British Library.

Printed in China

Title page: Alfred Wallis, *Five Ships – Mount's Bay* (detail, see page 19)

Acknowledgements and picture credits

For generous assistance in locating works and providing images, the author and publisher wish to thank: Sebastiano Barassi, Kettle's Yard; Catriona Colledge, Austin/Desmond Fine Art; Robert and Lucy Dorrien-Smith; Arwen Fitch, Tate St Ives; Anthony Hepworth; Katie Herbert, Penlee House Gallery & Museum; Simon Hucker, Jonathan Clark Fine Art; Simon Martin, Pallant House Gallery; Natalie Rigby, Falmouth Art Gallery; Patricia Singh, Beaux Arts London; Toby Treves, and the Vicar, Breage Church.

Thank you to the following for kind permission to reproduce copyright material on the pages listed: Arts Council Collection, Southbank Centre, London/Estate of David Bomberg, DACS, 93; Ashmolean Museum, University of Oxford, 109; Austin Desmond Fine Art/Artist's Estate, 58–9; Austin Desmond Fine Art, London, 107; Beaux Arts and the artists' estates, 65, 82, 99; Estate of Sandra Blow/Wescotts Quay Gallery, 92, 104; Bowness, Hepworth Estate/Tate, London 2011, 22, 106; British Council Collection/ Angela Verren Taunt, DACS, 69; Judy Buxton, 52; Richard Cook, 108; Richard Cook/© Estate of Partou Zia, 56; David Messum Fine Art, 85; Mary Fedden/Portland Gallery, 77; Ralph Freeman, 105; Anthony Frost, cover, 60; Anthony Hepworth, 100; Estate of Patrick Heron/DACS, 91; Jonathan Clark Fine Art/Estate of Roger Hilton, DACS 64, 84; Rose Hilton, 85; Estate of Bryan Ingham/Jonathan Clark Fine Art, 47; Kurt Jackson, 38; David Kemp, 83; Kettle's Yard, University of Cambridge (photographer Paul Allitt), 1, 19, 36; Andrew Lanyon, 34, 102; Matthew Lanyon, 86; Sheila Lanyon/DACS, 24, 49; Christopher Laughton, 5, 32, 51, 90; The Leach Pottery, 16; Felicity Mara, 63; Louise McClary, 46; Lee Miller Archives, 75; Cedric Morris Estate, 20; Estate of Bryan Pearce, DACS, 96; Penlee House Gallery & Museum, 30, 54, 55, 66, 67; Penlee House Gallery & Museum & Cornwall Studies Centre, Redruth, 10, 41; Penlee House Gallery & Museum/© Bridgeman Art Library/ Artist's Estate, 11; Roland Penrose Estate, 44; Oliver Plante, photography, 77, 78, 95; Port Eliot Collection/Plymouth City Council (Museums & Archives), 40; Royal Institution of Cornwall (RIC), 7, 15, 42; RIC/Artist's Estate, 73; Tate, London, 4; University of Chichester, Otter Gallery/© Estate of William Scott, 2011, 68; Estate of Walter R. Sickert/DACS, 12; Estate of John Tunnard (Clody Norton), 48; University of Nottingham/© Reproduced with permission of The Estate of Dame Laura Knight DBE RA 2011. All Rights Reserved, 72; Angela Verren Taunt/DACS, 43; Estate of John Wells/Jonathan Clark Fine Art, 76; Estate of Karl Weschke, 80; Estate of Bryan Wynter, 88; Jonathan Clark Fine Art, Estate of Bryan Wynter/ DACS, 89. Every effort has been made to trace copyright holders; any errors or omissions are regretted, and will be corrected in reprints and new editions on notification to the publisher.

Note

Measurements are in centimetres, height before width.

Plymouth by stagecoach took several days, and once you crossed the Tamar, the roads in Cornwall were notoriously poor. It was usually quicker to go by sea, skirting the coast, although this route also had its disadvantages. Cornish inshore waters had a fearsome reputation for shipwrecks. A couple of years before Turner's visit, the naval sloop *Primrose* foundered off the Lizard peninsula, with the loss of almost all of its crew of 127. This was only one incident among countless others – there was no avoiding such hazards.

Turner's mission was to paint watercolours of places he visited *en route*, which would then be turned into a book of prints, *Picturesque Views on the Southern Coast of England*. There was a strong market for this kind of publication. The country was at war with Napoleon's continental empire, and pictures conveying the nobility of the British landscape had a suitably patriotic aura. In the 1800s there were other reasons, too, why landscape had become an artistic subject with genuine mass appeal – an appeal that was to prove exceptionally deep and long-lasting. The industrial revolution of the eighteenth century, which set Britain on the path to becoming an overwhelmingly urban society, stimulated a craving for scenes of wild and open landscapes, in which humans were

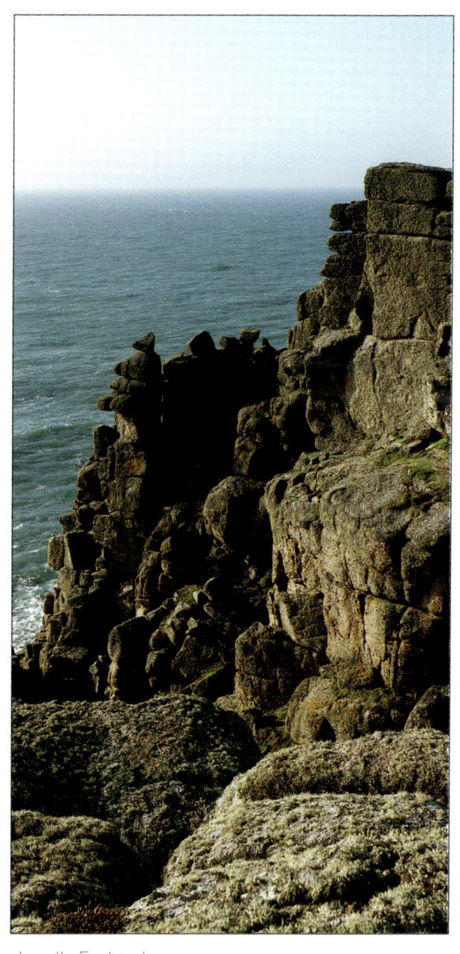

Land's End today

either absent or dwarfed by the splendours of nature. Coastal landscapes, with their horizon-wide perspectives, moved viewers – so the Romantic poet Shelley thought – because we feel that such places are 'boundless/As we wish our souls to be'.

In Turner's engraving of Land's End (page 4), storm-light shafts across a gunmetal sea on to the headland's sinewy contours and tombstone cliffs. Boulders in the foreground resemble teeth in a gigantic jaw. Published in 1814, also the year of Jane Austen's country-house novel *Mansfield Park*, this print represents a powerful, primitive landscape that will effortlessly shake off any attempt to tame it. Most viewers admiring Turner's image at the time would have been no more likely to visit Cornwall in person than they would the Amazon or the Sahara.

Present-day feelings are very different. A recent tourist marketing campaign portrays Cornwall as a Garden of Earthly Delights, where 'tantalizing views of deep wooded valleys and wide vistas of sparkling blue sea' create a 'luxuriantly coloured landscape'. The granite cliffs and reefs (page 5) are no longer feared as a deathtrap for hapless mariners but instead provide 'a naturally thrilling adventure playground'. The heavy industry whose sights, sounds and smells filled the air in Turner's day has all but vanished.

In the eighteenth and nineteenth centuries, travellers to Cornwall were struck less by the landscape's tantalizing luxuriance than by the pervasive stench of fish that greeted new arrivals in the coastal villages and, inland, by the dominant presence of the metal-mining industry. Large tracts of countryside were covered by waste heaps thrown up by tin, copper and arsenic mining. Coal smoke from pump-house chimneys and smelting furnaces drifted across cliffs and hillsides and through streets, along with the din of beam engines, millwheels and the massive mechanical hammers, or stamps, that crushed the ore.

The hellfire vitality of Cornwall's industrial revolution glows in the background of a double portrait painted by Turner's older contemporary, John Opie, in 1786 (page 7). Born in the mining village of St Agnes on Cornwall's north coast, where his father was a mine carpenter, Opie was a self-taught painter who became a fashionable portraitist in the academic style of Sir Joshua Reynolds. Known on the London art scene as 'the Cornish Wonder', Opie eventually became a professor at the Royal Academy, as did Turner shortly after him.

On the right of the portrait sits Thomas Daniell, wearing the old-fashioned powdered

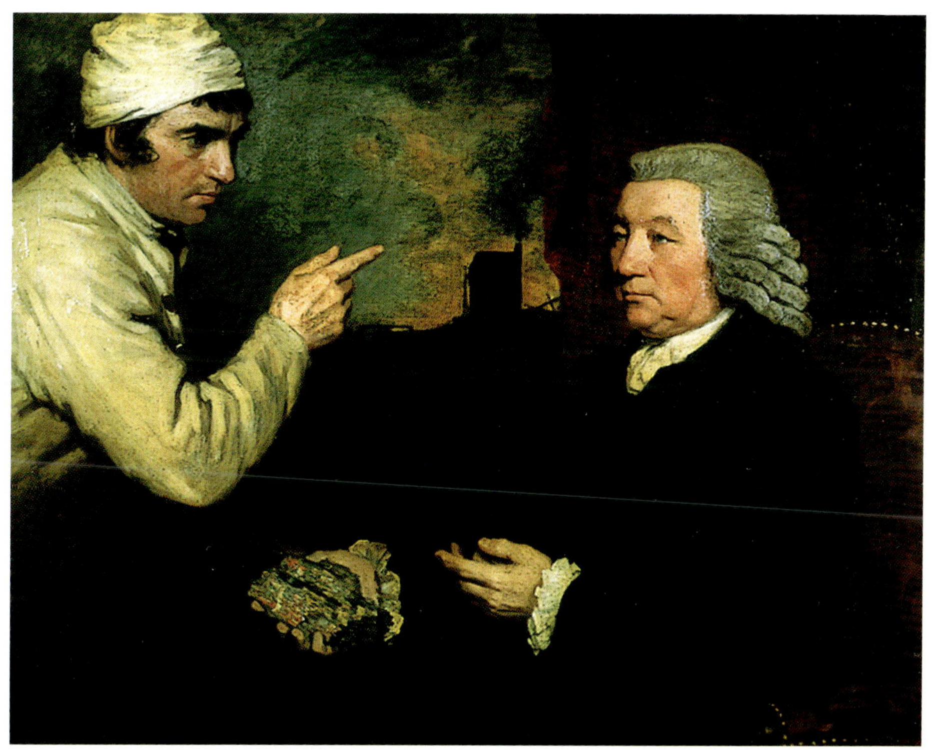

John Opie, A Gentleman and a Miner (Captain Morcom and Thomas Daniell), *1786. Oil on canvas, 99.5 x 112 cm*

wig of a gentleman-entrepreneur and grasping a lump of copper ore, the source of his wealth. The man on the left in workman's overalls is probably the mine captain, or superintendant, Thomas Morcom, who later worked with Richard Trevithick, testing the latter's innovatory steam-powered pumping equipment at St Agnes. Trevithick went on to develop the high-pressure steam technology that was to drive Victorian railways, shipping and factories. Opie's portrait catches the historical moment when Cornwall seemed every bit as likely to be taken over by machinery and tall chimneys as Birmingham or Stoke-on-Trent.

In the event, as the nineteenth century progressed, the Cornish mining industry ran into trouble – lack of local coal had always been a problem, and there was competition from overseas sources of tin. Instead, Cornwall increasingly became a place where people travelled to escape the expanding cities and factories in parts of Britain with better infrastructure and access to raw materials. The earliest vacationers were few and well-to-do, like Sir Leslie Stephen, father of the novelist Virginia Woolf and artist Vanessa Bell, who in 1881 took the lease on Talland House on the outskirts of St Ives. In Woolf's novel *To the Lighthouse*, which draws on her childhood memories of the late Victorian era, St Ives is already the haunt of artists, who could be seen any day setting up their easels around the harbour. The town remained the family's summer retreat until 1895, by which time, to Stephen's rather snooty dismay, the Great Western Railway was delivering regular trainloads of holidaymakers.

The railway had been built to serve Cornish industry, reaching Penzance in 1852, but it soon found another market in the growing tourist trade. How, though, could you entice passengers beyond the old-established West Country seaside resorts in Dorset and Devon to the far end of Cornwall, which lacked the elegant promenades and beachfront hotels of Weymouth or Torquay? The answer was to market a myth. Cornwall's tourist amenities were as yet pretty rough and ready, but to compensate for this its landscape could be clothed in Romantic allure. Cornwall was billed as 'home of the wild and imaginative'; the reality of travelling hundreds of miles to be marooned by drizzle in a Tintagel hotel could be magically transformed by tales of the Round Table and the Lady of the Lake. The vision of Cornwall as a foreign land, not really part of England at all, was seized on by the fledgling tourist industry. The catchphrase 'the English Riviera' cast a veil of Mediterranean glamour over a region struggling with economic decline. Early railway posters advertised Cornish sun, sea and *signorine* on the bizarre basis that the long, knobbly peninsula resembled a map of Italy.

Tourists were not the only expectant passengers the Victorian railways brought to Cornwall. Their arrival in ever-growing numbers towards the end of the nineteenth century coincided with the appearance of artists on the scene, not as isolated pioneers but as a steady influx. It was around 1880 that painters started to visit, and soon to settle in, the fishing village of Newlyn, next door to Penzance on the south coast of the Land's End peninsula. Several of them had already spent time in artists' colonies in the Dutch or French provinces, including Pont Aven and Concarneau in Brittany, where groups of urban painters such as Paul Gauguin lived among the local population. Like the Cornish seaside holiday, the European art colony movement was driven by nostalgia for the imagined simplicity and innocence of rural life. Artists sought out places where they felt that the landscape and people had not been corrupted by industrialization. They took their subjects from the way of life they observed around them, and often painted outdoors, or *en plein air*, a practice made possible by the invention of oil paint ready-mixed in metal tubes. The art colonists' work generally adopted a reflective mood and a muted, realist style, although here and there – most famously in Van Gogh and Gauguin's tempestuous colony of two in the Provençal town of Arles in autumn 1888 – real creative breakthroughs took place.

With its harbour thronged with sails and its fishy alleys clambering up the hillside into fields, Newlyn seemed just like an 'English Concarneau'. So thought the Irish painter Stanhope Forbes, who made his name at the Royal Academy in 1885 with a scene of a fish sale on the Newlyn foreshore. Forbes was a dedicated exponent of *plein air* painting. In one photograph he can be seen painting among the washing lines of Boase Street, Newlyn, where an older woman and a young girl pose for him, while other inhabitants look on amused (page 10). (The small picture on his easel is in the collection of Penlee House Gallery & Museum, Penzance.) An oil sketch Forbes made shortly after arriving in Newlyn shows a solitary working woman trudging across the sands, with the brown sails of fishing boats behind her out in the bay. This little work already has several of the ingredients for which the Newlyn School became celebrated (page 11).

The rail link to London made it practical for artists not merely to visit for a season but to become resident colonists. Walter Langley settled in Newlyn in 1882, to be followed by Edwin Harris, Fred Hall, Henry Scott Tuke, Forbes and his future wife, the Canadian Elizabeth Armstrong, and numerous others. Paintings were packed off in specially

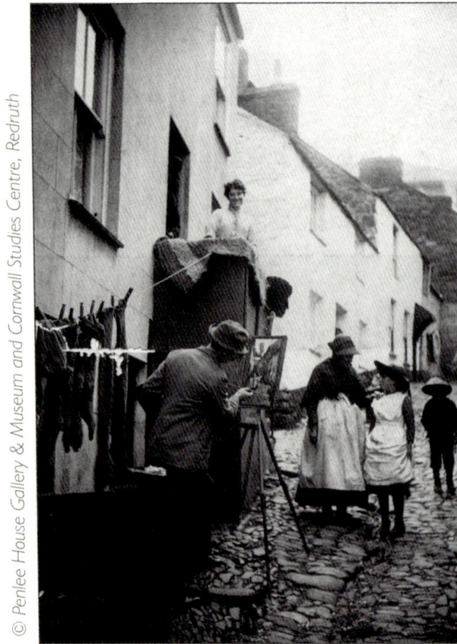

© Penlee House Gallery & Museum and Cornwall Studies Centre, Redruth

Stanhope Forbes painting in Boase Street, Newlyn (Newlyn Artists Photograph Album, 1880s)

chartered train carriages to be exhibited in London. For the first time it became possible for an artist to build a professional reputation while living in Cornwall. Newlyners, meanwhile, supplemented their meagre earnings by posing for the 'gentlemen artists'. They modelled for paintings of pretty young widows, apple-cheeked children and old folk worn to noble decrepitude. In such paintings the scarcity of young men – who, being out with the fishing fleet or down the mines, were less often available to pose – allowed male viewers to respond with pleasantly protective feelings towards the sitters. Hence, in part, the popularity of Newlyn School paintings with the Victorian public.

Around the same time, over on the north coast ten miles away, painters were converging on St Ives for slightly different reasons. Here it was the harbour town itself, the surrounding coastal landscape and the curiously luminous quality of the sea-light that attracted artists, rather than the arduous but picturesque lives of the local population, as in Newlyn. The American-born painter James McNeill Whistler, accompanied by younger artists Walter Sickert and Mortimer Mempes, stopped off in St Ives on a painting trip in the winter of 1883–4. Famous for his sensuous nocturnes, Whistler had recently returned from working in Venice. 'Nature,' he announced, 'contains the elements, in colour and form, of all pictures, as the keyboard contains the notes of all music.'

An oil sketch by Sickert, *On the Sands, St Ives* (1883), shows a young family enjoying a deceptively sunny winter's day on Porth-

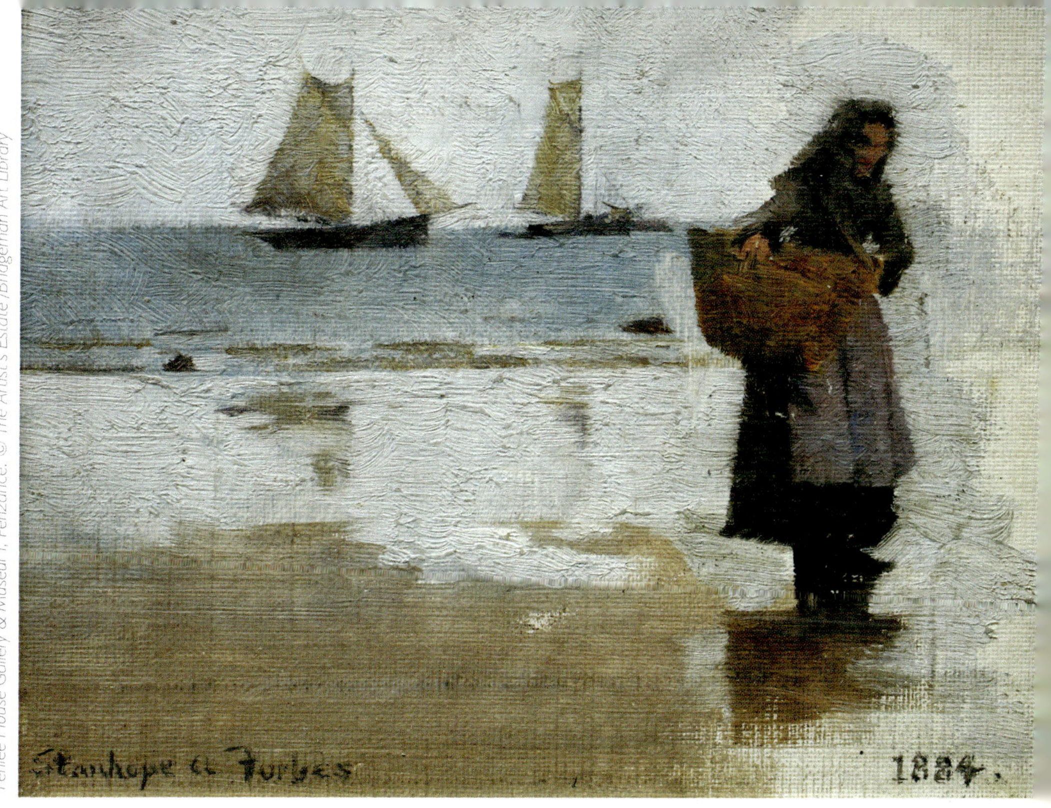

Stanhope Forbes, Study of a Fisherwoman, *1884. Oil on canvas board, 15 x 20 cm*

meor Beach (page 12). Comparing this small painting to Forbes's sketch on the Newlyn foreshore, you feel immediately the difference between artists' responses to Newlyn and St Ives. Where Forbes emphasized cloudy weather, toil and melancholy, the family in Sickert's scene inhabits a relaxed, leisure-time world, more like the French coast as seen through the eyes of contemporary Impressionist artists. By European standards, in fact, Newlyn artists were already old-fashioned, harking back to realist paintings of

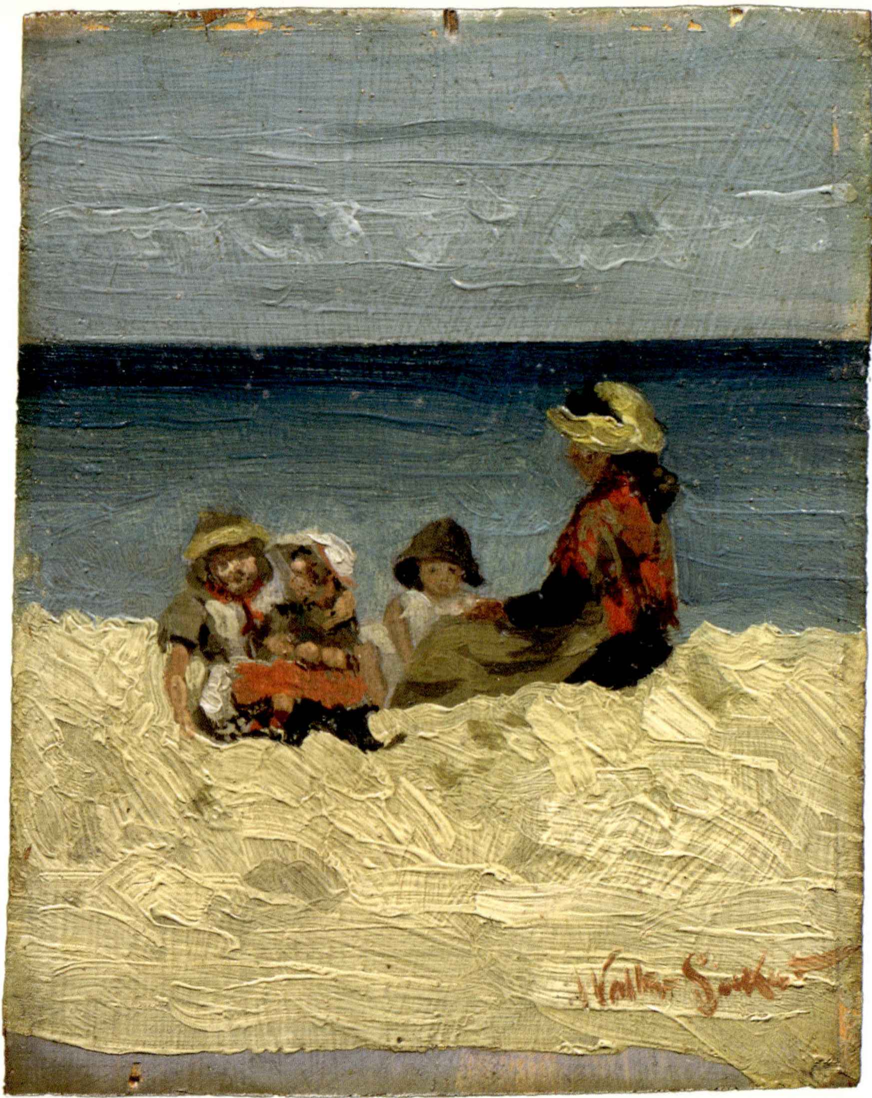
Walter Sickert

agricultural poverty by Jean-François Millet and Jules Bastien-Lepage. Sickert, by contrast, had absorbed the more recent Impressionist manner (he met Degas shortly before coming to St Ives), with its fleeting interplay of light and shade. The light at St Ives obviously had an effect on him. Sickert's housekeeper used to tease him about the drab London browns and greys for which his work was known by dipping his brushes in mud. To prove that he could lighten things up, he made her a gift of *On the Sands*.

By 1890 artists were acquiring old net and sail lofts to serve as studios, and Cornwall's thriving art colonies were being touted in guidebooks as a visitor attraction in their own right. In the background to this frenzy of painterly activity and railway tourism, an economic catastrophe was underway, with the collapse of west Cornwall's metal mining and pilchard fishing industries. Despite the dire industrial outlook, however, there were opportunities to be seized, as the Cornish-born press baron and doughty philanthropist John Passmore Edwards was quick to realize. Passmore Edwards funded libraries, art galleries and other public buildings throughout his native county. In May 1895, in his foundation-stone speech at Newlyn Art Gallery, he predicted that, although 'the mines of Cornwall were drying up', this old industry might be superseded by a new one based on Cornwall's 'scenic wealth' rather than its mineral deposits. In an early statement of what came in the 1990s to be termed the 'creative economy', Passmore Edwards saw the painters of Newlyn 'illustrating and interpreting that wealth in line and colour on canvas and thereby benefiting themselves, Cornwall and the world'.

Facing page: Walter Sickert, On the Sands, St Ives, *1883. Oil on panel, 14.6 x 11.8 cm*

So it was that in Newlyn and St Ives, art became deeply embedded in the community. More than anywhere else in provincial Britain, the business of art and the strange habits of artists were assimilated into the daily lives of local people. But the high enthusiasm and sense of common purpose of the early Newlyn School days tailed off through the 1900s. Some artists drifted away to pursue their careers elsewhere. Others stayed on, producing a steady stream of paintings in their traditional realist manner. Stanhope Forbes remained in Newlyn, where he and his wife Elizabeth founded a school of painting that continued for more than 40 years. In early twentieth-century London, meanwhile, audiences were busy being outraged by the exhibitions of recent (or fairly recent) French art staged by the artist and critic Roger Fry. People might prefer Forbes's kindly portraits of bearded old mariners to the mask-like sensuality of Gauguin's faces, but no one could claim they were modern.

In the end, though, it was the horrors of modern warfare rather than modern art that put an end to the colonists' convivial way of life in west Cornwall. Mass conscription during the First World War (1914–18) made no distinction between urban and rural in its hunger for young blood. Now that almost every family was losing its menfolk, the grieving mothers and fishermen's widows of Newlyn School paintings were less appealing subjects. It was at this time that the high moorland west of St Ives – a landscape that had so far received little outside attention – took on an unlikely new role. These scrubby uplands, where farming hung on amid an ancient network of stone-walled fields and defunct mines, became one of twentieth-century Britain's most celebrated destinations for artists and writers in search of freedom and self-discovery. It began in 1915, with the arrival of D.H. Lawrence and his aristocratic German wife, Frieda. Lawrence was looking for a place to work unharassed after his latest novel, *The Rainbow*, had been banned and publicly burned in London. As the February gorse burst into flower around him, he declared the landscape around Zennor 'the best place I have been, I think'. It was a savage Eden, where, for the moment, he felt safe from the hypocrisies of middle-class morality and aggressive militarism. Here he could begin again.

Soon enough the authorities forced Lawrence and Frieda, who was technically an enemy alien, back to London. And after the war, when artists began to return to Cornwall, no one was much in the mood for innovation or unconventionality. Painters such as Borlase Smart, who had made many drawings of the Western Front trenches where he served, settled down in St Ives to paint the less traumatic drama of the elements. In Smart's *Morning Light, St Ives* (page 15) the academic manner of 1900s British art is leavened by lighter atmospheric colour and a vivid, snapshot sense of the framed instant learned from Impressionism. Smart's mentor and another prominent artist in St Ives between the two world wars was the Danish-born Julius Olsson, who specialized in high-angle views of moonlight blanching the ruffled waters of St Ives Bay (page 102).

By 1920 the belief that the arts could make a useful contribution to Cornwall's fragile

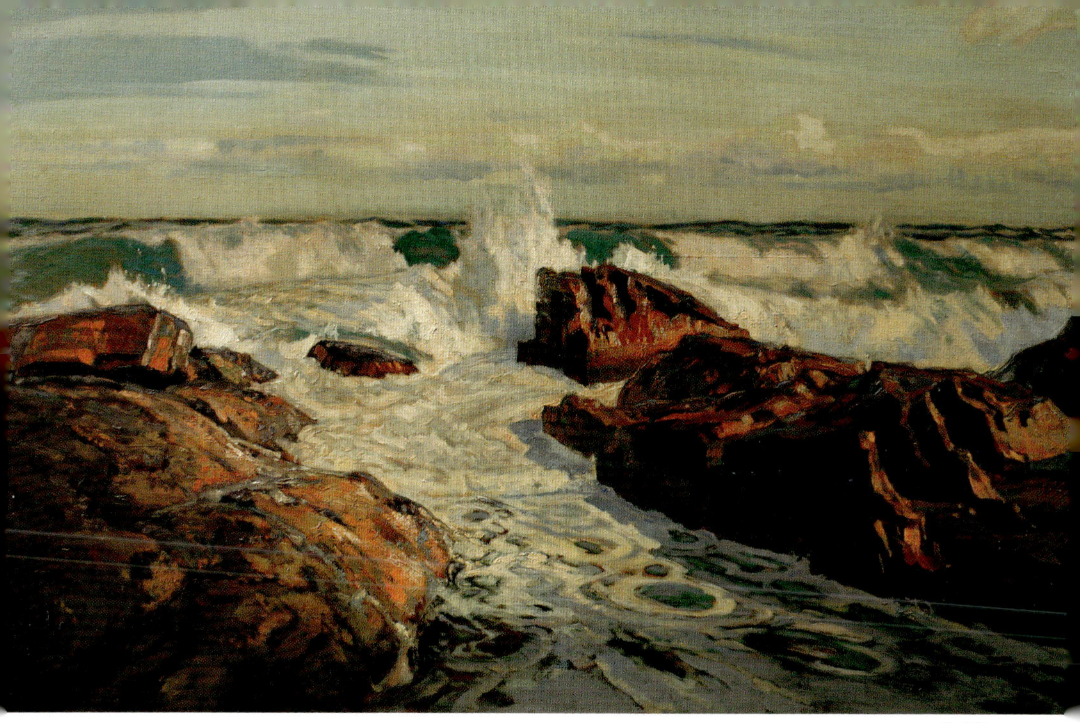

Borlase Smart, Morning Light, St Ives, *1984. Oil on canvas, 88 x 129 cm* © RIC

post-industrial economy had taken root. In this year Frances Horne, wife of a wealthy rice trader living near St Ives, advertized for a potter to join her scheme for stimulating local employment through craft production. What she got was Bernard Leach, newly returned to England from Japan, with his gifted assistant Shoji Hamada. Leach had become something of a celebrity in the Japanese folk craft movement (yet another response to disenchantment with industrialization and urban living). He and Hamada constructed an oriental kiln on the outskirts of St Ives, where Leach put into practice his vision of a meeting between East and West in the potter's craft, producing vessels based on oriental and medieval models. He believed that the practical yet harmonious shape of a

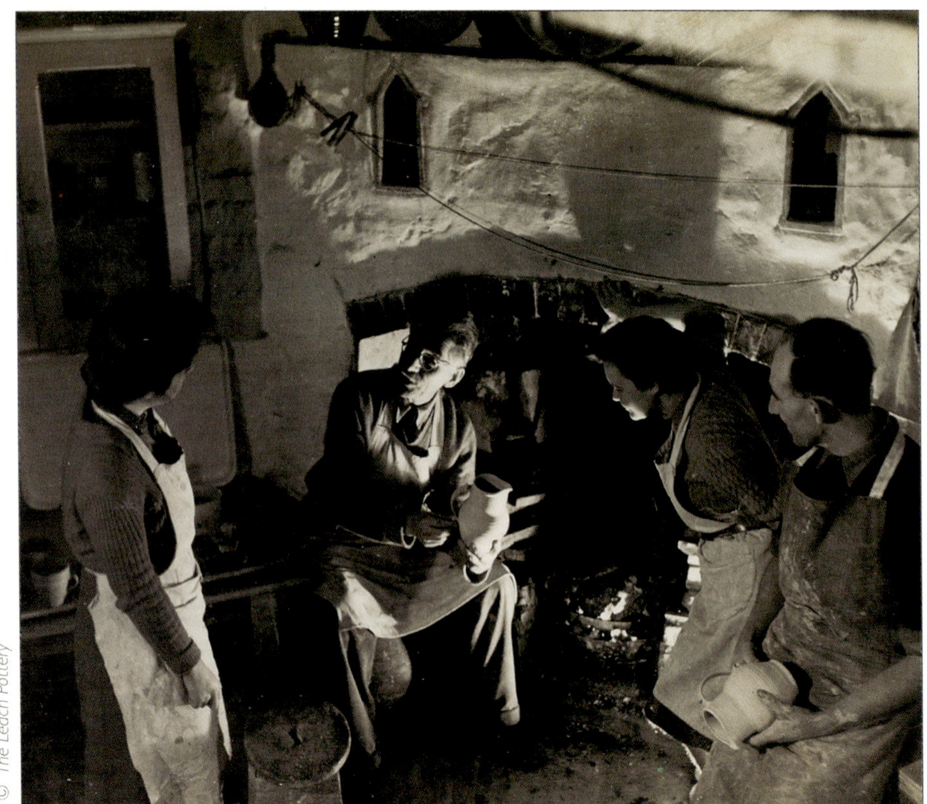

Bernard Leach with students and his son David (right) at the Leach Pottery, St Ives, c.1949

well-made and decorated pot reflected the maker's spiritual outlook. An inspirational mentor – though a hopeless businessman – Leach passed on this vision to generations of student-disciples. His advocacy of the dedicated life of the artist-craftsman gradually became a distinctive element in the ethos associated with St Ives.

If Leach saw himself as the prophet of a new creative dawn, the same could not be said about the rest of the Cornish art scene in the 1920s. The painters of conventional harbour scenes and seascapes saw little point in doing things differently, though names from the wilder shores of contemporary European art such as Picasso, Matisse or Dalí must have reached even St Ives. Art and tourism continued to go hand-in-hand: aside from robust romantic landscapes, Olsson, Smart and other painters in Cornwall had a useful sideline designing railway posters. Then, in August 1928, came the first, quite accidental contact between art in Cornwall and progressive, modern painting.

Among the holidaymakers down from London that summer were Winifred and Ben Nicholson, who shared a waterside cottage near Truro with some Hampstead friends and a young Paris-based painter, Christopher (Kit) Wood. Wood and the Nicholsons belonged to a group of young artists whose ambition was to 'begin again in painting'. They wanted to counteract the muted colours and stuffy conventions of much British art of their day, to look with a fresh eye, like early Renaissance Italian artists or self-taught painters such as 'Douanier' (customs officer) Rousseau, who was then much in fashion in Parisian avant-garde circles. Winifred Nicholson believed that, in the 'new world' their art looked forward to, there would be 'no false ornament – but clarity, white walls, simplicity – complete and satisfying'.

During their stay, Ben Nicholson and Wood made a day trip to St Ives, where Wood had holidayed two years earlier. Here, as Nicholson recalled, 'on the way back from Porthmeor Beach we passed an open door… and through it saw some paintings of ships and houses on odd pieces of paper and cardboard nailed up all over the wall, with particularly large nails through the smallest ones. We knocked on the door and inside found [Alfred] Wallis.' Wallis was then in his seventies. His working life had taken him from hired hand in the Newfoundland fishing fleet to small-time dealer in marine salvage, with a shop on the quay in St Ives. After the death of his much older wife, Wallis had started painting 'for company'.

The paintings that so enthused Nicholson and Wood weren't the accomplished products of marine artists, in which neither of them had any interest, but deceptively childlike images of ships under sail and dreamlike bird's-eye-view harbour scenes (page 19).

Into these paintings Wallis focused a startling intensity of memory and observation, set down with a highly distinctive technique. He painted on anything that came to hand – often cardboard packaging and irregular bits of wood, but also crockery and furniture. He preferred boat and house paint to artists' oil colours, proudly observing, 'I use real paint. Not like the paint artises [artists] use.'

This chance meeting was to have lasting repercussions for the work of Ben and Winifred Nicholson, Wood and their circle, who eagerly spread the word about Wallis, and for the future story of art in Cornwall. Not that anyone visiting St Ives in the 1930s would have noticed much change in tempo among its resident artists, who viewed Wallis as merely an eccentric local character. For the Nicholsons and Wood, meanwhile, the currents of their lives soon took them elsewhere. In 1930 Wood, whose opium addiction was undermining his sanity, died falling (or jumping) under a train at Salisbury station. Shortly afterwards the Nicholsons' marriage foundered, following Ben's affair with the sculptor Barbara Hepworth, whom he was to marry in 1938.

In the 1930s, while Ben and Barbara's London circle of progressive artists still admired Wallis, their main focus was on Paris and the abstract work of such European artists as Mondrian and Brancusi. Although few people would have thought the words 'modern art' and 'Cornwall' belonged in the same sentence, individual avant-garde artists continued to settle there, including the abstract artist Marlow (born Marjorie) Moss in the early 1920s and the Surrealist painter John Tunnard, who moved to the Lizard peninsula in 1933. Cedric Morris, like the Nicholsons and Wood a member of the 7&5 Society, lived briefly in Zennor; his painting of a ramshackle cliff-edge industrial installation (page 20) is in many ways more typical of the local landscape than the popular romanticized versions. On the whole, these artists kept their ties with the wider art world and had limited involvement with the traditional art colony scene.

Then in 1939, with war in Europe imminent and the threat that London would soon be bombed from the air, the history of modern art once again (and again almost by accident) connected with Cornwall. Two more of Nicholson's Hampstead friends, the writer Adrian Stokes and his artist wife Margaret Mellis, decided to move to safety near St Ives. Here in late August they were visited by Nicholson, Hepworth and their young triplets. When war was declared a

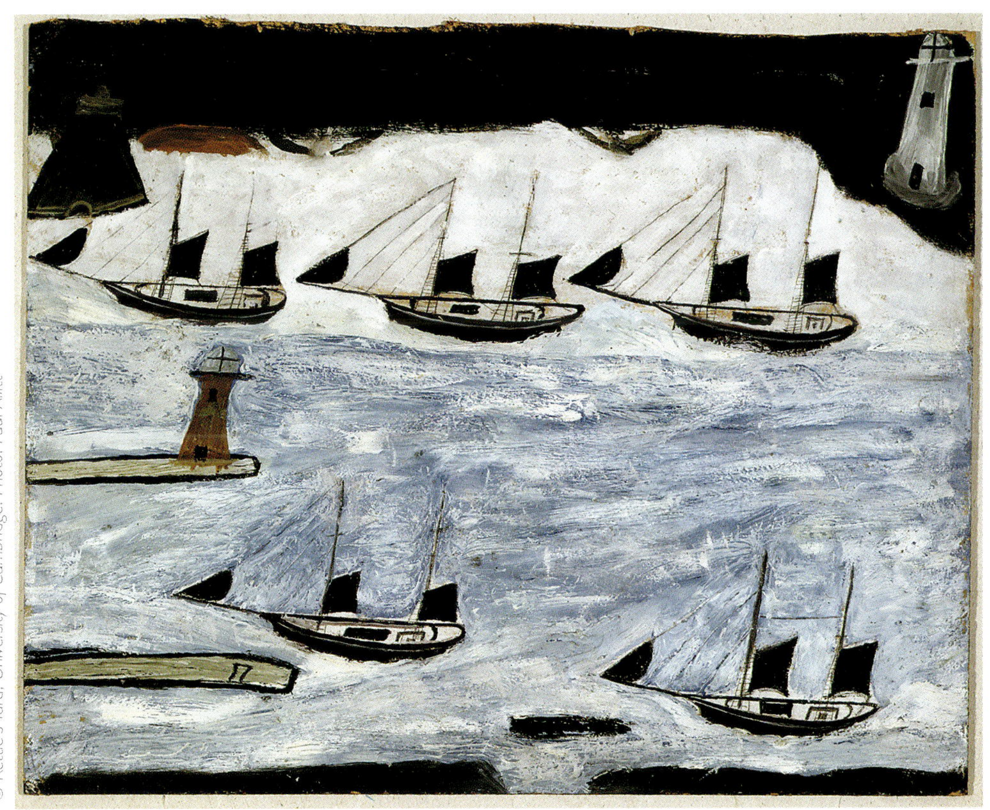
© Kettle's Yard, University of Cambridge. Photo: Paul Allitt

Alfred Wallis, Five Ships – Mount's Bay, *c.1928. Oil and graphite on card, 44 x 55.5 cm*

few days later, Ben and Barbara stayed put, and quickly persuaded the émigré Russian sculptor Naum Gabo and his wife, Miriam, to join them in their Cornish exile. In the 1930s these artists had all been involved in a Europe-wide abstract art movement, whose

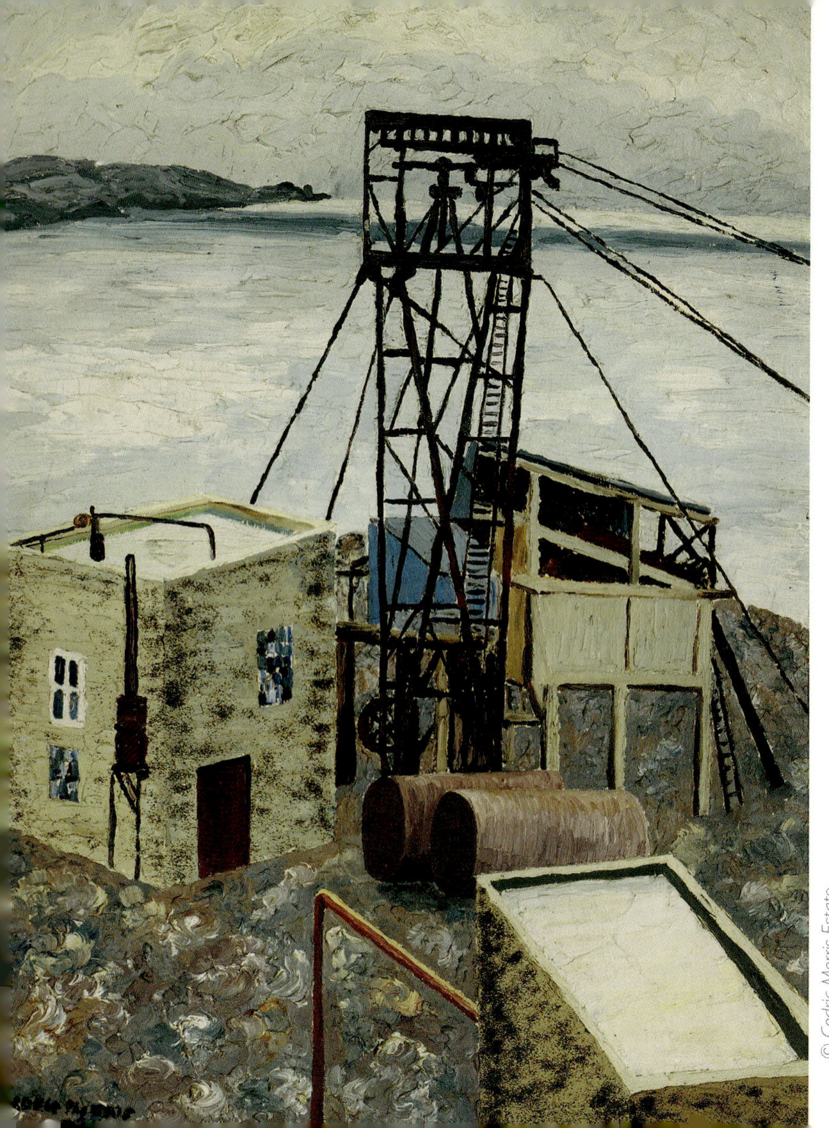

ultimate aim was to transform people's ways of seeing and living – a utopian ideal that was passionately opposed to fascism. Gabo's experiments in what he called 'Constructive art' went back to the years following the Russian Revolution, when the new Communist government briefly enlisted avant-garde artists in its social and economic reforms. During the war years in Cornwall, 1939–45, it was difficult for this small group in St Ives to pursue full-scale work, but the exchange of ideas continued. They kept in touch with other artists, some of whom also decamped to Cornwall, including Wilhelmina Barns-Graham, a fellow student of Mellis's from Edinburgh School of Art, and John Wells, who spent the war working as a doctor on the Isles of Scilly.

Although none of these artists had planned to end up in Cornwall, they found that aspects of their adopted environment struck a chord with their existing ideas. Hepworth became enthralled by what she saw as the abstract and universal sculptural qualities of west Cornwall's geology. She wrote of the view across St Ives Bay, 'The rock formation of the great bay had a withinness of form that led my imagination straight to the country of West Penwith behind me – although the visual thrust was straight out to sea. The incoming and receding tides made strange and wonderful calligraphy on the pale granite sand that sparkled with felspar and mica.' This landscape seemed to have been shaped by forces of nature just as stone or wood are carved by a sculptor. There was, Hepworth increasingly felt, a mysterious connection between the landscape in which she lived and the forms that preoccupied her in her art. She said that the strings in her 1946 wood sculpture *Pelagos* (page 22) were intended to express 'the tension I felt between myself and the sea, the wind or the hills'.

Nicholson, meanwhile, renewed his contact with Wallis, now very old and suffering from dementia but still painting (he died in 1942). It was more than a decade since that first meeting, but Nicholson again found the shapes and colours of the Cornish landscape seeping into even his most geometrical paintings. Under pressure to produce work for sale, he drew and painted small representational landscapes in something like his earlier, Wallis-inspired manner – 'potboilers' he called them – in the hope that they might attract buyers in the conservative climate of wartime. For the twenty-one-year-old Peter Lanyon, who was born in St Ives and began

Facing page: Cedric Morris, Landscape, Cornwall (Quarry), *1923. Oil on canvas, 61 x 45.7 cm*

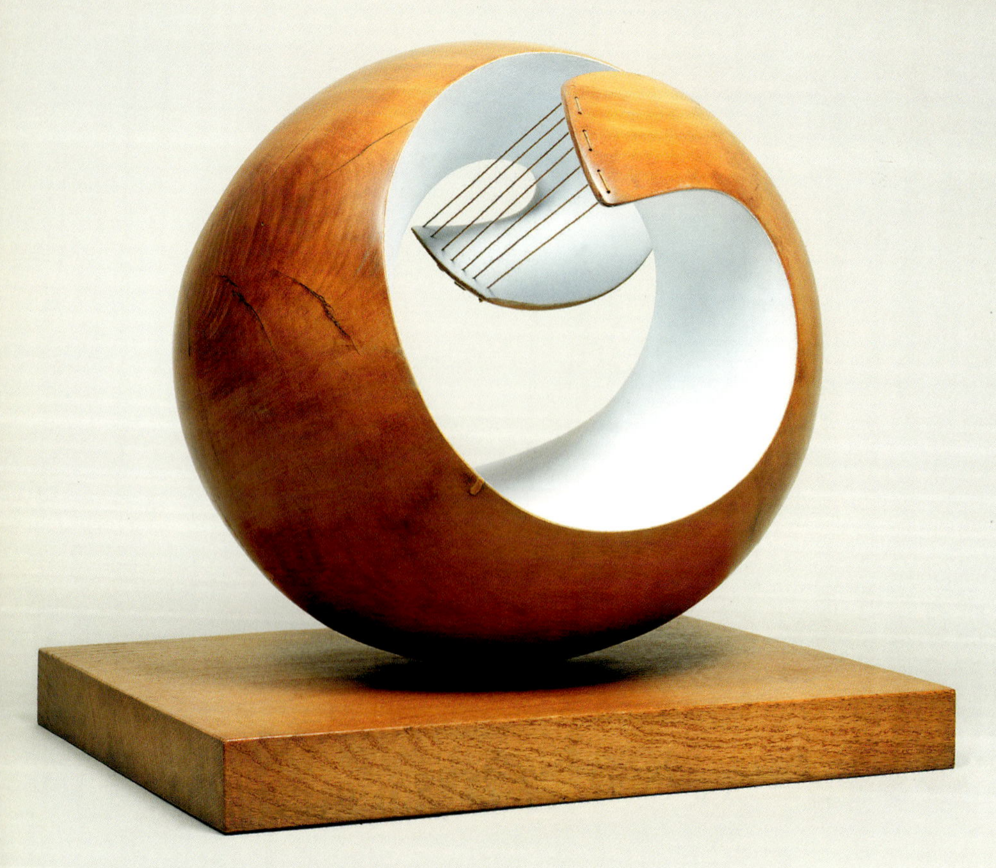

Barbara Hepworth, Pelagos, *1946.*
Part-painted wood and strings, 43 x 46 x 38.5 cm

his art training at Penzance School of Art and with Borlase Smart, contact with Nicholson, Hepworth and Gabo (before he was called up into the RAF) transformed his sense of what was possible for an artist working in Cornwall.

When the war in Europe ended in May 1945, you'd have expected Nicholson, Hepworth, Gabo and their little nucleus of avant-garde companions to return without delay to their former lives. In the event, although Gabo soon emigrated to the USA, Nicholson was to remain in St Ives until 1958, when he left for Switzerland, while Hepworth stayed on a further 30 years until her death in 1975. They found that they could keep up with their network of professional contacts from Cornwall as well as anywhere, and the visual stimulus that they'd discovered in the landscape around them promised new ideas for work.

It was at this point that the next phase began in the story of modern art in Cornwall – the most vigorous and unprecedented so far. As millions of servicemen and women were demobbed during 1945–6, young artists congregated in and around St Ives. Their experiences of the past six years varied greatly: for some there had been the trauma of front-line combat or long imprisonment, for others the enforced tedium of menial duties on the home front. The sense of starting again, of at last being able to get on with their lives and work after six years of war, was infectious and intense. There was no question in people's minds of simply going back to the way things had been in 1939 – in art as well as in politics.

On a personal level, artists headed for Cornwall for all kinds of reasons. Lanyon, for example, was returning home. Once back in St Ives, he began to develop his own interpretation of abstract art, which fused geometric ideas with the forms and textures of his native landscape. Responding to some of Gabo and Hepworth's abstract sculptural themes, he made three-dimensional constructions related to his painting process (page 24). Terry Frost, meanwhile, had served as a commando and spent four years in a prisoner of war camp in Germany, where he'd started painting. His work was noticed by an artist and fellow inmate, Adrian Heath, who had – as it happened – studied with Stanhope Forbes in Newlyn before the war. Heath told Frost that, if he was serious about becoming a professional artist, St Ives would be a good place to start. No one can have realized just how many new arrivals there would be in St Ives after the war – many of them wanting to work in modern idioms that were com-

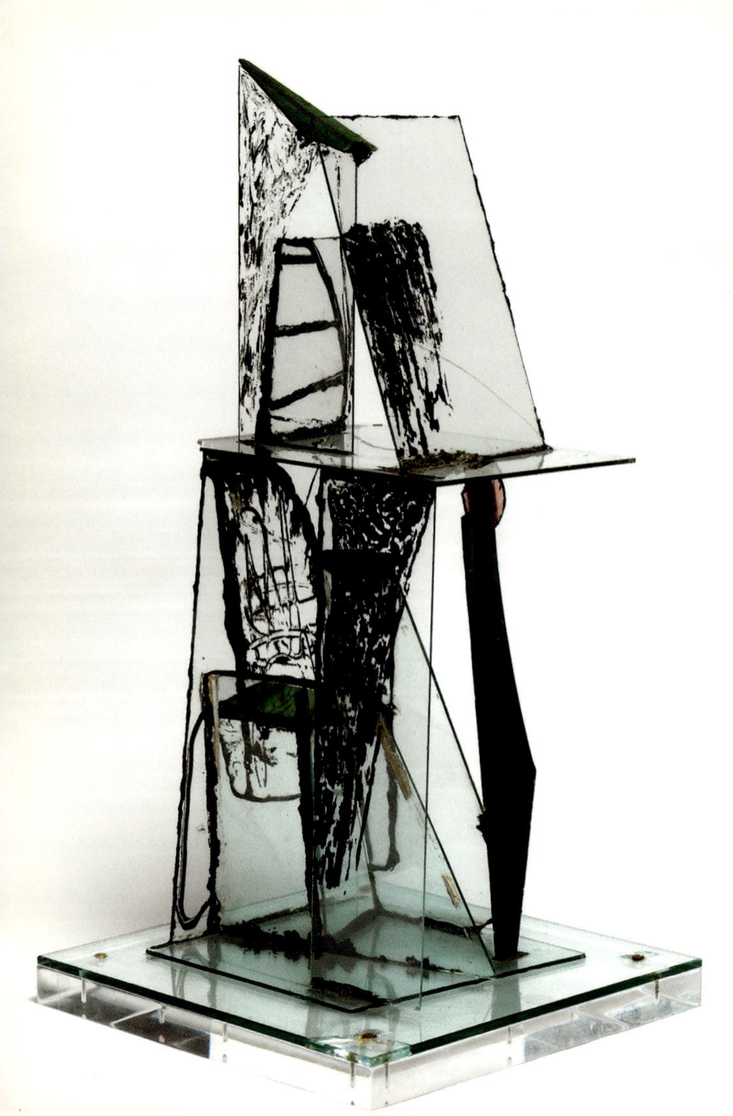

Peter Lanyon,
Construction for St Just,
1953. Mixed media,
65.3 x 28.4 x 25.5 cm

pletely different from the art usually associated with the town. John Wells, Bryan Wynter, Denis Mitchell, Wilhelmina Barns-Graham, Patrick Heron… so many artists converged there in the 1940s, from different places and backgrounds. This was the time when people began to talk about St Ives as one of the main centres of modern British art.

Young artists didn't always head for Cornwall because of any particular interest in, or even knowledge of, Hepworth or Nicholson's work. They had their own ideas. Yet these older artists' well-established national and international contacts made St Ives a place where you could hope to start a professional career. Officials from the Arts Council, which arranged exhibitions of contemporary art throughout the country, and the British Council, which promoted British artists' work abroad, were often to be seen around St Ives. So was Herbert Read – critic, curator, poet and something of an art-world grandee. Read had championed Nicholson and Hepworth's work in the 1930s; in the late 1940s he was perhaps the best-connected ally a British artist could have. In 1948 he agreed to become the first president of the newly formed Penwith Society of Artists.

Between about 1946 and 1960 west Cornwall could claim a significance in modern British art that is unique for such a small, rural region so far from the metropolitan art world. At one time or another, a high proportion of the leading modern artists, especially painters, in Britain passed through St Ives. They include artists who lived and worked in the area for many years, such as Barns-Graham, Frost, Heron, Lanyon and Wynter, and others who touched down comparatively briefly, among them William Scott, Francis Bacon and Sandra Blow.

In the mid-1950s Patrick Heron, who was an art critic as well as a painter, played a crucial role in building the reputations of younger artists in Cornwall. His articles in British and American journals advanced the idea of a modern 'St Ives School' whose values were shared by a number of his contemporaries (none of whom, in reality, much liked the idea of being so closely identified with St Ives). In 1956 Heron moved down from London to west Cornwall; for the previous ten years he had spent most summers in St Ives. In his writings he was an eloquent advocate for the work of Lanyon, Frost, Wynter, Alan Davie and other young painters. All were engaged in abstract painting, though not of the austerely geometric kind practised by Nicholson and Gabo in the 1930s. Instead, like their contemporaries in France and the USA, they put great importance on the expressive quality of an artist's brushmarks and the sense of movement in the way paint was applied. The terms gestural or action painting, Abstract Expressionism or the French word *tachisme* are often used for this kind of work.

Heron was convinced that British abstract painters were just as original and impressive as their counterparts in the USA, such as Jackson Pollock and Mark Rothko, but that they suffered from not having the commercial and political weight of the New York art world behind them. Nevertheless, there was a moment when Heron felt it was true to speak of a 'St Ives–New York' axis. In the late 1950s and early 1960s Hepworth, Nicholson, Frost, Wells, Heron and Lanyon, among others, had exhibitions in the USA, while Rothko and the influential critic Clement Greenberg both visited Cornwall. Heron recalled that the New York dealer Martha Jackson had plans to turn an old building on Porthmeor Beach (near where Tate St Ives now stands) into a waterfront art gallery to rival Peggy Guggenheim's palazzo on the Grand Canal in Venice.

By the early 1960s this moment had passed. In New York Abstract Expressionism was pushed out of the limelight by Pop art. In London a comparable fashion shift was underway. To many people abstract painting seemed hard to understand and far too serious. A new generation of British artists were producing paintings that took a critical view of contemporary society but were also figurative, wacky and colourful in a way that gave them much wider, easier appeal. The work of David Hockney and his contemporaries felt closely in tune with 1960s youth culture and consumer society – something that was difficult for artists around St Ives who had been young in the decade before the Second World War, and were geographically isolated from urban trends. On the London gallery scene, painters identified with the modern 'St Ives School' fell out of critical favour.

In Cornwall, meanwhile, the artistic community still seemed to be thriving. Curious to see what was going on, younger artists were constantly turning up throughout the late 1950s and 1960s. After meeting Frost in Leeds, Trevor Bell motorbiked down in 1955 and found a cottage to rent at Higher Tregerthen, where D.H. Lawrence had lived 40 years earlier. Next door was the young German-born painter Karl Weschke, who had been interned as a POW in Eng-

Facing page: Trevor Bell painting in Porthmeor Studios, 1958

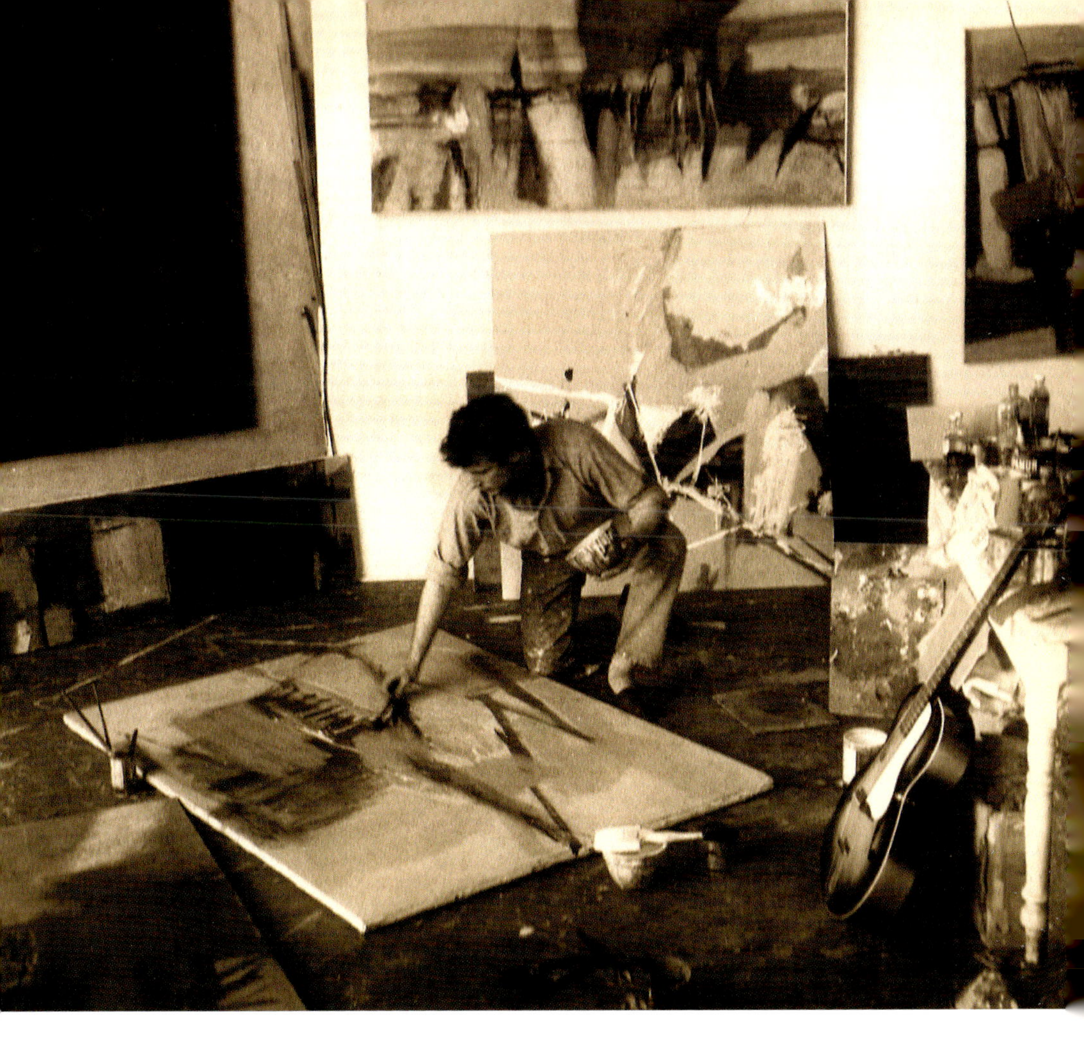

land and was making a precarious living as a lion-feeder in a London circus when Bryan Wynter met him and encouraged him to join the west Cornwall crowd. Jo Tilson and Peter Blake, who are now firmly associated with British Pop art and never thought of in terms of 'St Ives', were among many artists who lived for a time in west Cornwall or just passed through. Roger Hilton bought a run-down cottage at Nancledra, a few miles inland from St Ives, which the minimalist painter and sculptor Bob Law had been renting from Trevor Bell. And so the area's art life went on regenerating itself.

The social climate of the 1960s in Cornwall was summed up by Hilton's son Matt: 'Those young painters [Frost, Lanyon, Wynter] were a bit like jazz musicians, they had this edge to them, and a lot of them were snappy dressers – my father was a very snappy dresser – and Patrick Heron was pretty cool. You've got to throw yourself back into all that Beat stuff to get a sense of all these artists, in their 20s and 30s, even 40s... driving around in jeeps. It was like a movie going on when we went down to Cornwall. A kind of glamour and turbulence.'

For artists emerging from the experience of the Second World War, Cornwall had been a place that, in some irresistible yet unaccountable way, chimed with their hopes. Its landscape wasn't picturesquely rural, like Sussex, or grandly wild like the Lake District; it felt as though it had been both damaged and strengthened by its industrial past. Yet the mechanized destruction of the war had left it almost untouched. Its society was small-scale, but it had a long seafaring history of contact with other worlds and wider horizons. Twenty years on, the extraordinary sense of challenge and release that marked the immediate post-war period had lost its edge. For a younger generation west Cornwall's appeal was more as a bohemian refuge. In the early 1960s St Ives, like other British seaside resorts, was a magnet for beatniks – a place where, in the days before cheap air travel, you could experience something like a Californian atmosphere of beachside creativity and suntanned counterculture.

At the same time, the avant-garde art of the 1940s and 1950s had become part of the tourist landscape – something visitors associated with Cornwall and expected to see there. Abstract Expressionistic paintings vaguely reminiscent of Lanyon; colour compositions paying homage to Heron, or Nicholson-style abstract paintings proliferated in galleries throughout Cornwall. In St Ives the elderly Hepworth was a kind of civic celebrity, whose trademark holed sculptures were symbols of the town and its artistic heritage. Several of her studio assistants, such as John Milne, went on to make careers in their own right, though few shook off the influence of Hepworth's massive, nature-inspired abstract forms (Bob Law was a rare exception).

There were still cheap studios as well as congenial society to be found, especially for artists looking for a place to work outside the urban art world. As Breon O'Casey, who moved to St Ives in the early 1970s, observed, 'They talk about artists being attracted to St Ives because of the light. That's all balls: it was the sense of camaraderie against an at best indifferent, at worst hostile world that drew them.' Being in a place where, in contrast to most British provincial towns, art was accepted as an occupation like any other, was 'like having a great burden taken off me'. By the 1970s, however, St Ives no longer commanded the interest of Arts Council opinion-formers or dealers eager to spot new talent. In practical terms, artists here and throughout Cornwall either had to earn a living by servicing the tastes of summer tourists (which meant pictures containing recognizable lighthouses, headlands, blue horizons and so on) or they had to make their reputations elsewhere. Of the few professional openings other than gallery sales, Falmouth School of Art under principal Michael Finn provided employment as its student population and numbers of staff increased through the 1960s.

Two artistic societies founded many years earlier – Newlyn Society of Artists (1895) and the Penwith Society of Arts (1948) – continued to attract a wide membership, buoyed by their history of serious artistic endeavour and the promise of large gallery spaces where members could exhibit. While the Penwith Society remained loyal to the abstract interpretations of landscape themes favoured under its early dominance by Hepworth and Nicholson, Newlyn Society of Artists was more heterodox. This was partly Lanyon's influence; after quarrelling bitterly with Hepworth and Nicholson in 1951, he chose Newlyn as his power-base for promoting a more inclusive idea of art. 'There are as many sorts of art as there are artists,' he wrote, in a heated correspondence with Herbert Read, 'but there still remains Art.'

Lanyon's insistence that there should be no dogmatic distinction between 'modern' and 'traditional' was echoed in the pluralist artistic middle-ground – part-figurative and part-abstract – occupied by many of the painters whose work could be seen at exhibitions in

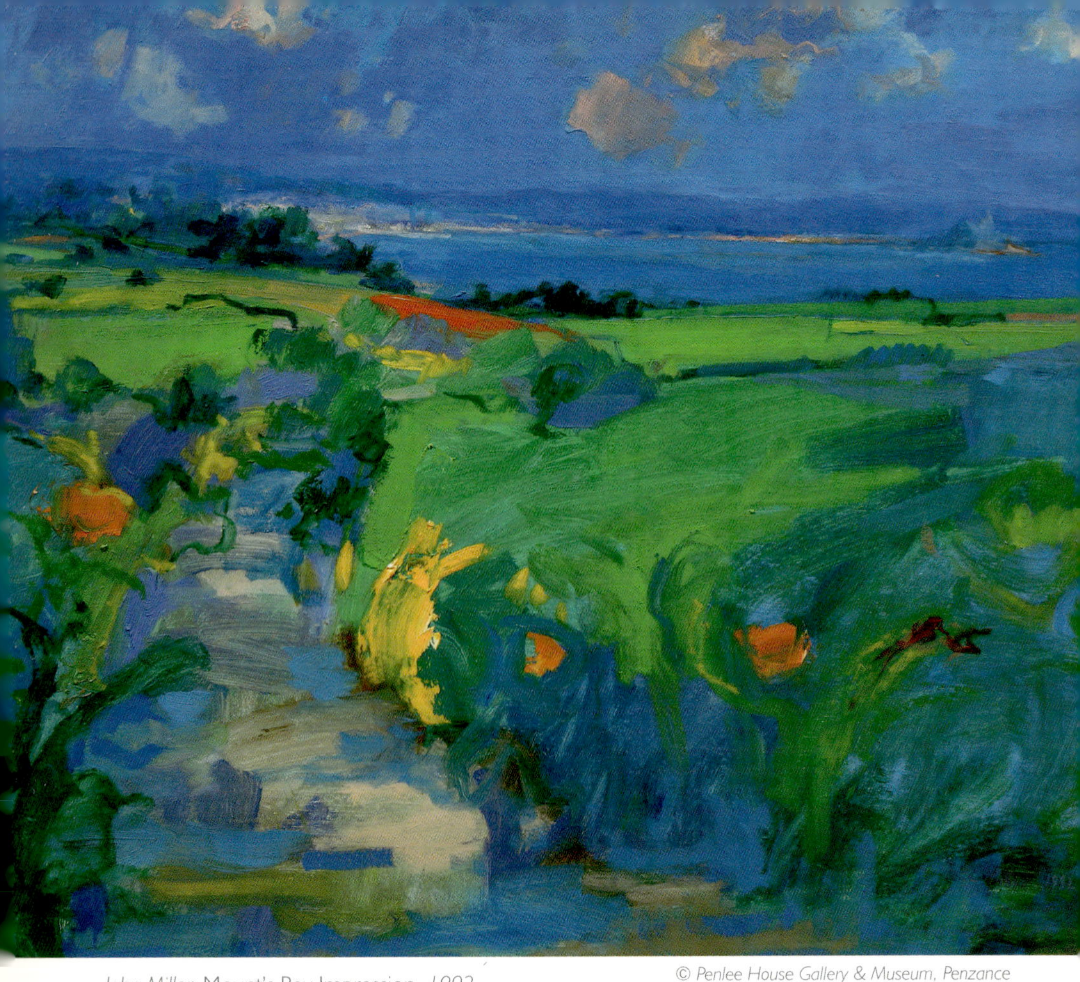

John Miller, Mount's Bay Impression, *1992.*
Oil on canvas, 75 x 90 cm

Newlyn and St Ives from the 1960s to the 1990s. They included the former architect John Miller (page 30) and the Mousehole-born Jack Pender, both of whose work combined references to earlier modern art with local landscape. After 1975, however, it became increasingly difficult to claim that anything very new was going on in Cornwall. That year saw the deaths of Wynter, Hilton and Hepworth. They weren't the last of the post-war generation: Frost returned from a decade in the Midlands to live in Newlyn in 1974, and Wells, Barns-Graham, Weschke, Paul Feiler and other artists continued to live nearby. To outside observers, however, the creative and intellectual dynamo that had been turning since the 1940s became distinctly weaker with each passing year.

In Britain more generally, it's true, the 1970s were marked by a growing pluralism and uncertainty about the future direction of art. The old divisions (abstract/figurative, oils/watercolour, painting/sculpture) gave place to a diversity of new approaches that had emerged during the 1960s, such as performance, conceptual art, video and installation. The 'end of painting' was repeatedly prophesied, as the whole notion of what constituted Art became far more fluid than it had been for Lanyon's generation. If it had ever made sense to speak of 'Cornish art' or a 'St Ives School', from the 1970s onwards such terms seemed largely irrelevant to artists' intentions. Where connections with Cornwall existed, they tended to be ignored or played down. Richard Long's *Cornwall Slate Line*, shown at the Tate Gallery in London in 1990, consisted of a fragmentary pathway constructed from splinters of Cornish slate. As a student in Bristol in the 1960s, where Lanyon occasionally lectured, Long had been impressed by the Cornish artist's theories of 'placeness' and his strategies for bringing the physical experience of landscape into art. His own slate line was constructed from the very geology of Cornwall, yet as an installation that could be reassembled in any large gallery space, it was also curiously placeless – in other words international.

In 1985 the story of modern art in Cornwall was given its most clearly defined form so far, when the Tate Gallery staged a large exhibition titled *St Ives 1939–64: Twenty Five Years of Painting, Sculpture and Pottery*. Including work by about 40 artists and actually covering most of the twentieth century, it marked the consolidation of 'St Ives' as a recognized category in art history, rather than simply the name of a small town where artists had happened to work. The show coincided

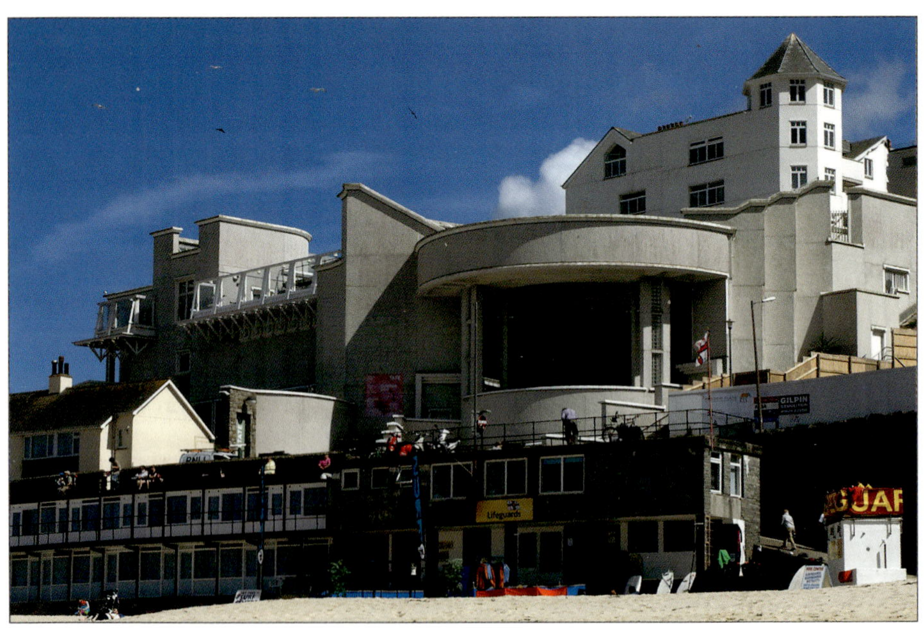

Tate St Ives from Porthmeor Beach

with the first discussions that would lead to the construction of Tate St Ives. The new gallery occupied the site of the old municipal gasworks overlooking Porthmeor Beach, across which Nicholson and Wood had been walking before their chance encounter with Alfred Wallis 65 years earlier. The opening in June 1993 coincided with the moment when Cornwall, like the rest of Britain, was tentatively emerging from the economic recession of the early 1990s.

Once again – much as Passmore Edwards had envisaged at Newlyn in the 1890s – art in Cornwall was seen to have a strategic role in the region's economy. The media attention attracted by Tate St Ives, with its striking location and architectural references to both 1930s abstract art and the forms and textures of old St Ives, helped the Cornish tourist industry to reinvent itself. Alongside its traditional bucket-and-spade image came an increasing emphasis on upmarket cultural and heritage tourism. The advent of National Lottery funding for arts and heritage in the 1990s also made possible big improvements for existing public galleries and museums in the region, such as Penlee House in Penzance and Falmouth Art Gallery.

A century ago, if you'd heard people talking about 'art in Cornwall', they would have been discussing the activity of outdoor landscape painting – a bracing business involving portable easels balanced precariously on harbour walls or planted in the sand. Now they would be more likely to mean looking at, rather than making, art – what's on in Cornwall's galleries and museums. Artists themselves, meanwhile, have mixed feelings about the use of 'Cornish' as a marketing label that inevitably associates paintings with pasties, ice-cream and other touted regional products.

Andrew Lanyon, eldest son of Peter Lanyon, has explored the strange ironies of this situation in his paintings (page 34), writings and films. In an extensive series of illustrated books, Lanyon has fictionalized the stand-off between art and science in a Cornish setting. Art, and especially abstract art, features in his stories as a virus that has impregnated the very air and soil – the 'art virus' you can catch simply by walking the streets of St Ives. And sometimes, among all the galleries and the flyers for exhibitions and open studios, and the Hepworth sculptures planted at strategic points around the town, it feels as though this really is what happens.

Lanyon reminds us that, for an artist, one of Cornwall's virtues is its refusal to separate art from everything else that is going on or to put it on a pedestal. You can't shake the sand and sea out of the history of art in Cornwall. I think of the great Russian sculptor Naum Gabo in his rented bungalow above the beach at Carbis Bay during the Second World War, determinedly fabricating a series of tiny geometric constructions from cardboard, string and Perspex, which he softened in the kitchen oven. He was convinced that the abstract ideas embodied in these home-made sculptures would one day, translated on to a much grander scale, shape the future of Western society. And as things turned out, Gabo was right – the ideas cooked up in his Cornish oven were to influence the shape of cities, buildings and designs after the war, and so to feature in the lives of millions (but that's another story).

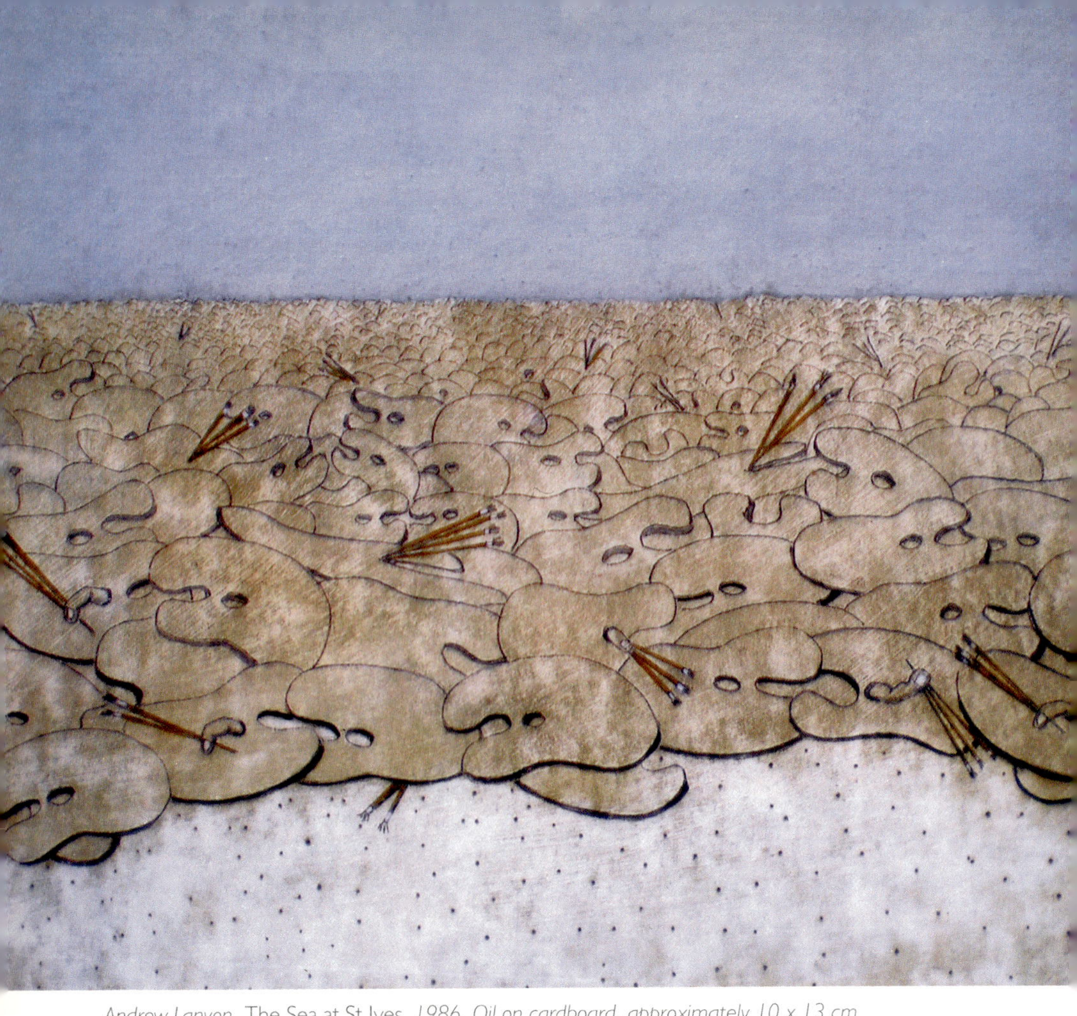

Andrew Lanyon, The Sea at St Ives, *1986. Oil on cardboard, approximately 10 x 13 cm*

Westwards from the Tamar

Although this book began as the story of art in Cornwall, its centre of gravity has already shifted to the peninsula's western extremity, the area lying roughly between Land's End, St Ives and Newlyn. For art historians Cornwall is often represented by this small area, further subdivided into the artists who worked in and around Newlyn and those in the orbit of St Ives. But Cornwall begins at the River Tamar, 70 miles or so from Land's End. There are places associated with art and artists that span its entire length, even if the party gets louder and more crowded as you travel west. This chapter and the next three chart a geographical and artistic route between the Tamar and the Isles of Scilly, looking at the ways in which different places are reflected in artists' work, sometimes in an easily recognizable form, sometimes in more allusive or abstract ways.

The naval dockyard town of Devonport, just on the Devon side of the Tamar, is where Alfred Wallis was born in August 1855 – as he liked to recall (inaccurately) on the day the Russian stronghold of Sevastopol fell in the Crimean War. The sights he remembered from his Victorian boyhood were to resurface in the paintings he made in old age in St Ives. He was only three years old when the railway bridge across the river to Saltash on the Cornish side was opened by Prince Albert in May 1859. Designed by the great engineer Isambard Kingdom Brunel, it established the first reliable and reasonably fast land route between Cornwall and the rest of Britain. Trains travelling upcountry were laden with metals, flowers and fish; those crossing the Tamar in the other direction were soon delivering tourists and landscape artists.

Resembling a gigantic metal sculpture straddling the Tamar at the point where it widens towards the sea, Brunel's single-track bridge is still the only rail link into Cornwall. Its arches form a long double curve, which appears to rise steeply as though being compressed as the train approaches, then flattens and lengthens as you look back. The Royal Albert Bridge's distinctive outlines feature in several of Wallis's paintings, transformed and heightened by memory but nevertheless unmistakable. In *Boats before a Great Bridge* (c.1935–7, page 36), painted as was Wallis's

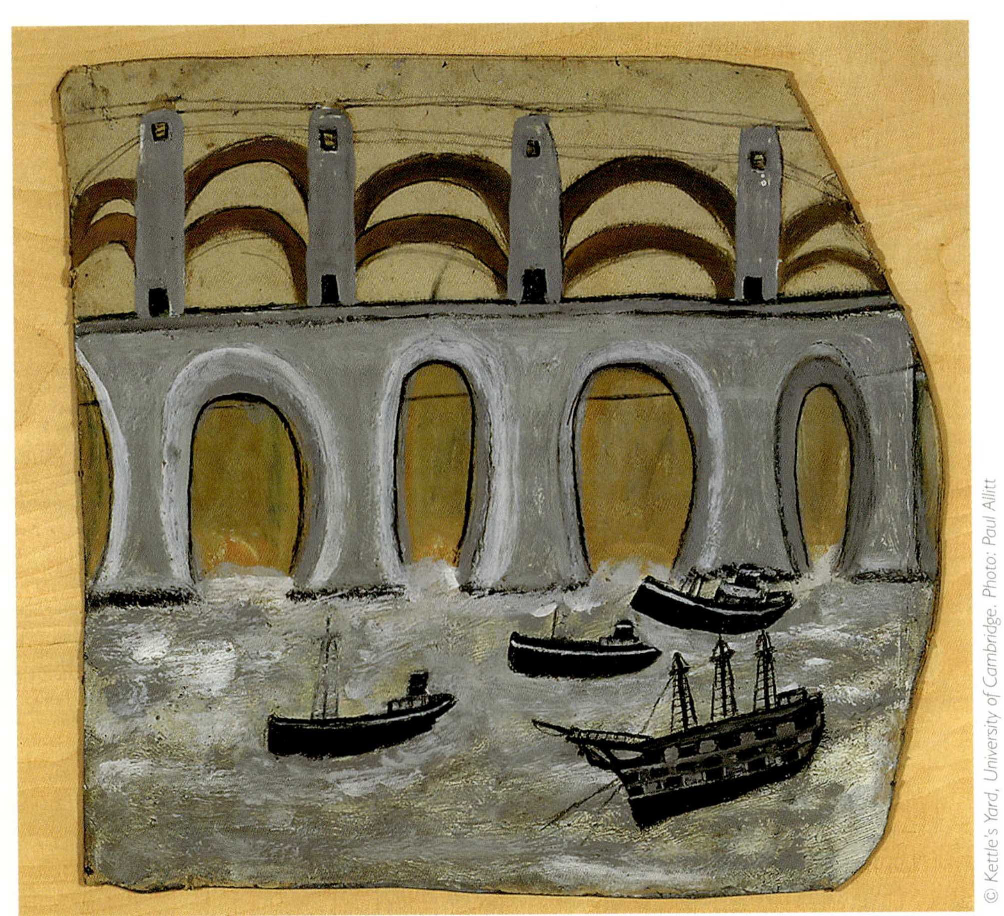

© Kettle's Yard, University of Cambridge. Photo: Paul Allitt

Alfred Wallis, Boats before a Great Bridge (Royal Albert Bridge?), *c.1935–7. Oil on card, 36.7 x 39.2 cm*

habit on an irregular piece of cardboard, the bridge has gained several arches and seems to be built of white stone, like an ancient temple. It rears over three steamboats – or perhaps just one steamboat at three different points along its journey – and what looks like a Nelson-era battleship moored in the estuary below, which echoes the ghostly presence of the vast white bridge.

Today Wallis's paintings of sailing ships, harbours and lighthouses have become an integral part of the way Cornwall is packaged for the wider world: they turn up on mugs, tea-towels, café menus and holiday websites. But the Wallis brand, with its innocent seaside appeal, belies a strange, otherworldly quality in his images. He once confided to a young relative that the outsize fish he occasionally showed swimming beneath or alongside his boats had a special meaning, that each boat 'had a soul, a beautiful soul shaped like a fish'. Wallis was about sixteen when the family moved to Penzance; he subsequently spent most of his life in St Ives. He took those memories of the Tamar with him, the estuary crowded with all the different types of vessels engaged in ocean-going, coastal and river-borne trade.

You don't have to travel far upriver today to leave behind the echoes of industrial and maritime activity, as the wide Tamar swings quietly between reedbeds and derelict quays. Whereas the Victorian landscape painters of Wallis's youth tended to turn their backs on the signs of industry, soothing their urban audiences with views of wild or pastoral countryside, contemporary artists are more conscious of the layers of human history beneath such scenes. In place of the machinery, muck and toil that earlier landscape painters swept under the greenery, they find a poetry of decay and loss. There's a sense of deep frontierland stillness in Kurt Jackson's series of paintings following the length of the Tamar Valley, where the river gleams reposefully in the dawn light or under an overcast sky. In *Rain, Cothele oaks and holly, Calstock viaduct* (2008, page 38), the wilderness seems to be reasserting itself, the marks of human presence dissolved to the distant reflection of the railway viaduct's arches. Jackson is alert to the way we mark nature with our imprint (the artist's hand and boot prints often feature in his paintings).

It's never long before the word 'landscape' finds its way into any discussion of art in Cornwall, although once you turn inland, away from the cliffs, coastal valleys and sea horizon, it isn't always obvious why the landscape in front of you exerted such a

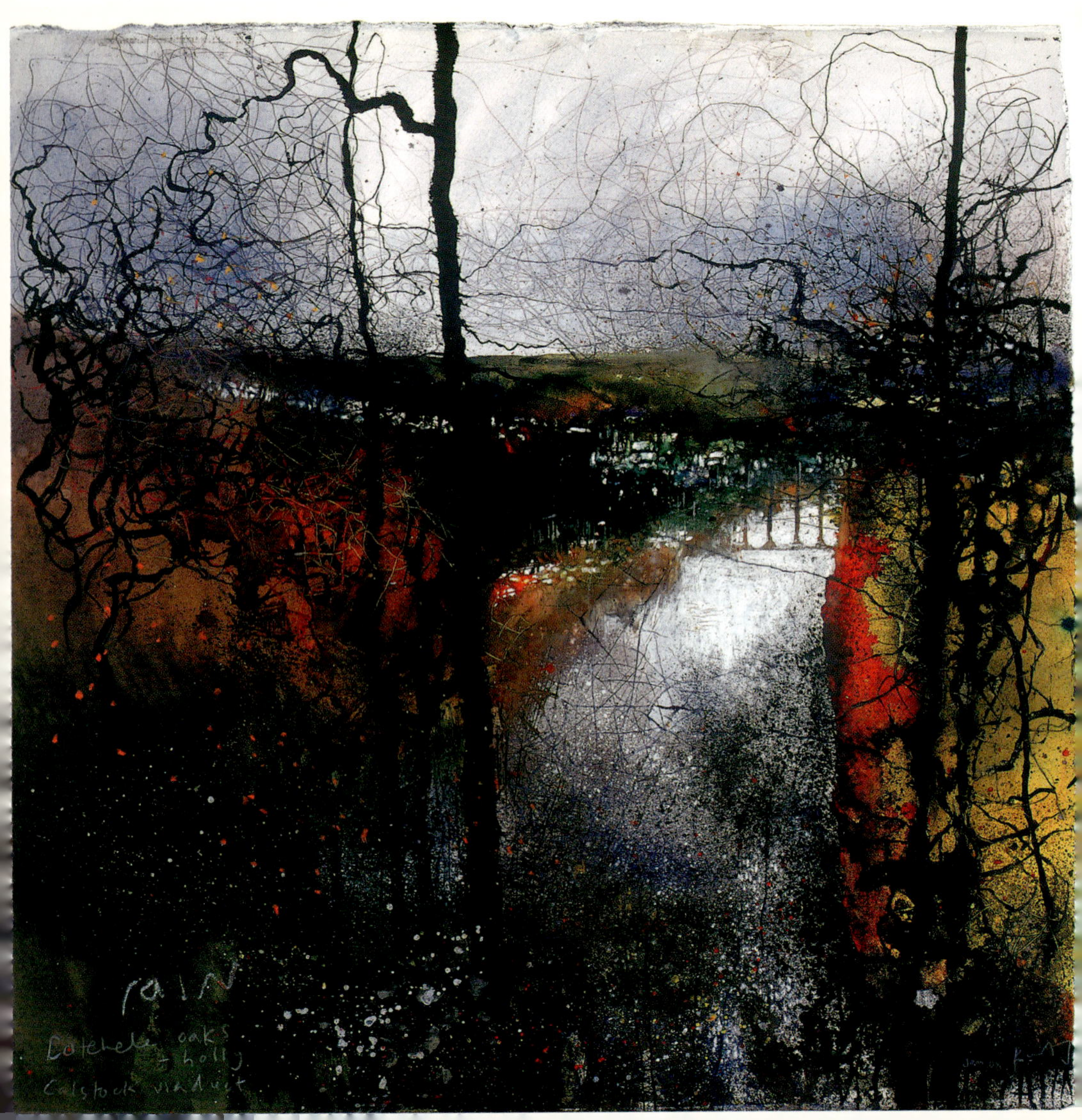
rain
Cotehele oaks
& holly
Calstock viaduct

hold on artists, in both their work and their words. 'Everyone in Cornwall talked about the bloody landscape,' complained Terry Frost, who arrived in St Ives as a recently demobbed serviceman in 1946, 'and I had to fight that.' What, asked Roger Hilton, who regularly rented studio space in Cornwall during the 1950s but didn't live there full-time until 1965, was 'all this tomfoolery about scenery' about? Something comparable had happened in the Lake District in the late eighteenth century. Up until then the Cumbrian mountains were simply mountains, but in the work of Romantic poets and artists they became metaphors for powerful, almost inexpressible experiences. And in the wake of the artists – as was later to happen in Cornwall – came tourists, eager to sample the sublime, mysterious power of landscape that poems and paintings had convinced them they would experience.

Apart from Turner's epic sketching tour to Land's End in 1811, however, the Cornish landscape was slow to catch on as a subject for art to compete with the Lake District or the mountains of Scotland and Wales. Before the arrival of painter-colonists from the 1880s onwards, in fact, 'art in Cornwall' mostly meant the kind of art with which country houses all over Britain were crammed. This consisted of family portraits, like the numerous works commissioned from Joshua Reynolds by the earls of St Germans at Port Eliot, near Saltash (page 40), alongside souvenirs of ancient Greece and Rome brought home from the Grand Tour, and Italianate landscapes in the picturesque style of the day. In other words, Cornish wealth from tin and trade was ploughed into much the same kind of art as fortunes made from Midlands coal, Lancashire cotton or West Indian sugar. What attracted the promising young Devon-born artist Reynolds and his contemporaries to Cornwall was the prospect of being paid to paint upper-class faces. It certainly wasn't anything as insubstantial as the quality of light or the spirit of place.

A century later the railway changed all this. When Victorian artists reached Cornwall, they usually gathered in coastal places not too far from a station, like St Ives or Newlyn (walking distance from the Great Western terminus at Penzance, page 56). The less easily accessible north coast, though equally scenic, didn't on the whole experience the same gentlemanly congregation of

Facing page: Kurt Jackson, Rain. Cothele oaks and holly, Calstock Viaduct, *January 2008. Mixed media, 57 x 57 cm*

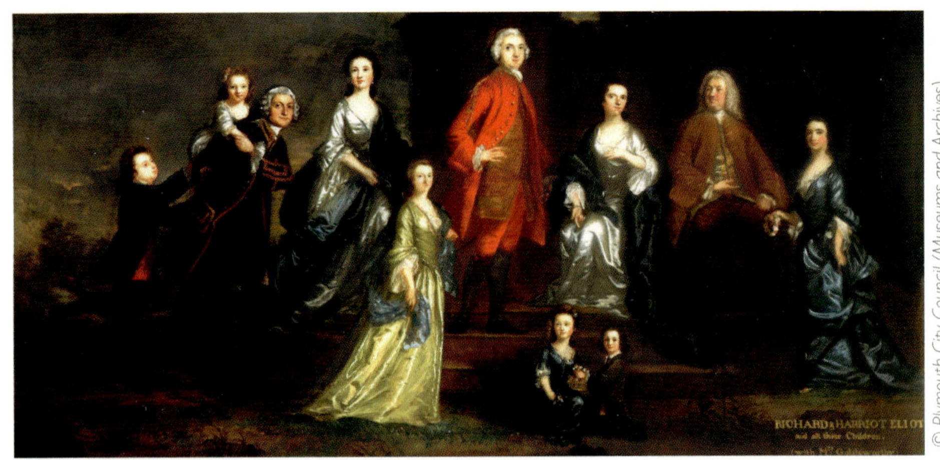

Joshua Reynolds, Richard Eliot and Family *(detail), 1746. Oil on canvas, 85.3 x 11.8 cm*

easels and palettes along its quaysides. And compared with the coast, inland areas of east and central Cornwall such as Bodmin Moor – the closest Cornwall gets to mountainous terrain – left only a passing trace in art. This is also true of the man-made plateaux that shape the landscape around St Austell to the south. These vast spoil heaps thrown up by kaolin extraction continuously grow and shift. Marked by the pyramidal forms of the older mounds and the intense, Caribbean blue of the mica-filled pools in exhausted workings, the landscape has a film-set strangeness, yet it doesn't fit with the popular idea of what Cornwall should look like. It was unusual for a Newlyn School artist to pay it much attention, as Harold Harvey did in the 1920s (page 42). For Harvey, a student of Norman Garstin (see page 55) and the only prominent Newlyn School artist to have been born in Cornwall, labour in the clay pits, boatyards and tin mines was as strong a theme as fishing-village life.

The River Fal rises in the wetlands of Goss Moor, on the fringes of the clay country, and runs south-west towards the coast, where it widens into a deepwater estuary indented by narrow creeks. In contrast to Cornwall's

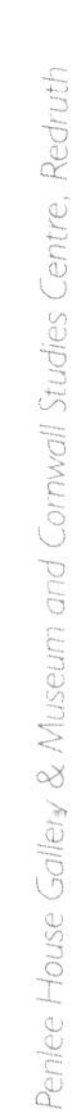

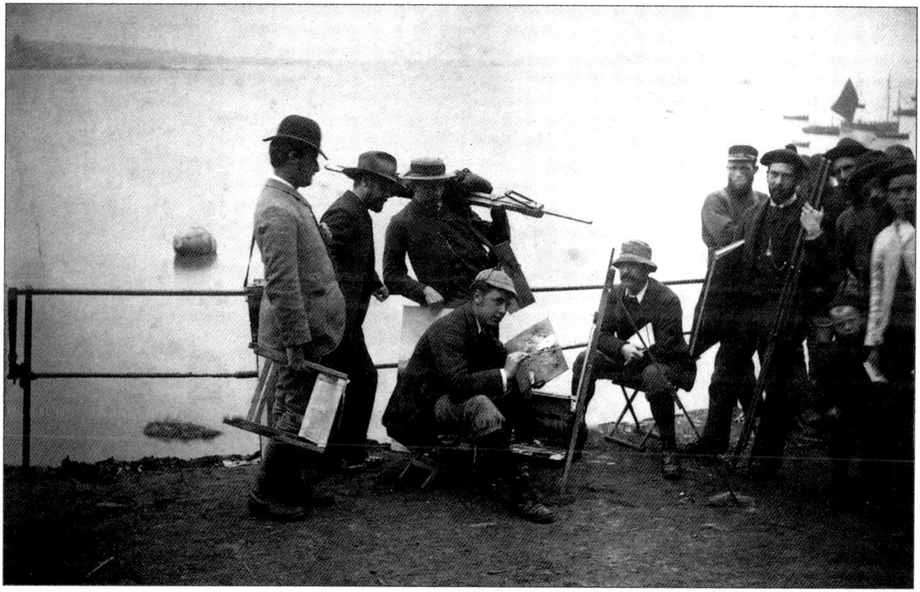

Artists on the cliff, Newlyn. L to R: Unknown, Walter Langley, Percy Craft; seated, Frank Bodilly (Newlyn Artists Photograph Album, 1880s)

treeless uplands, this riverine landscape is thickly wooded – private and introspective rather than open and exposed. With good sailing and fishing nearby, between the two world wars it became a favoured holiday hideaway for the urban élite, including two notable artistic house parties. It was beside Pill Creek, near Feock, that Ben Nicholson and Kit Wood were staying in August 1928, when they visited St Ives and encountered the aged Alfred Wallis. Nicholson produced a couple of little paintings of their immediate surroundings by the Fal. Sketchy and apparently unfinished, *1928 (Pill Creek, moonlight)* (page 43) is redolent of what Winifred Nicholson called the 'Sleeping Beauty' atmosphere of the place. Yet the contours of hillsides and the meeting of land and water are clearly drawn,

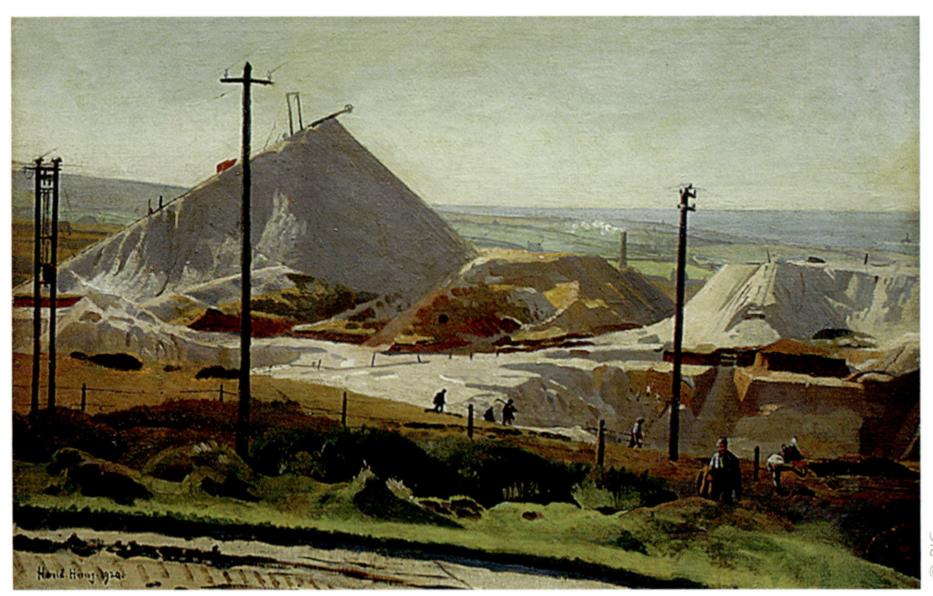

Harold Harvey, A China Clay Pit, Leswidden, *1920 or 1924. Oil on canvas, h. 76.2 cm*

so the dreamlike quality is balanced by something more detached and analytical.

The storybook feeling in Nicholson's painting seems innocent indeed when set beside mementos of a later party that took place in another secluded creek, near the confluence of the Fal and Truro rivers in July 1937. Here the artist and collector Roland Penrose hosted a wild week with guests from the world of European Surrealism. They included his new lover, the American model and photographer Lee Miller, and the artist Max Ernst, who was on the run from the police after his recent London exhibition had been shut down on grounds of obscenity. He'd been whisked off to Cornwall by Penrose, whose brother owned a bolthole there, Lambe Creek House. The party also included Ernst's twenty-year-old muse, the painter Leonora Carrington, the photographer Man Ray

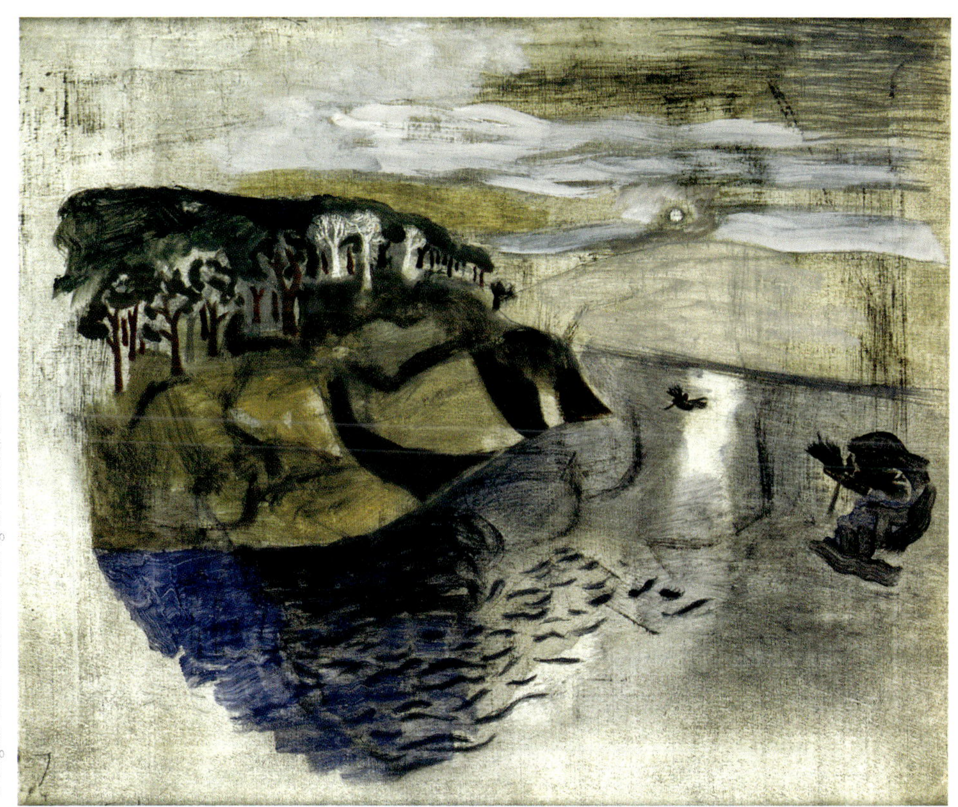

Ben Nicholson, 1928 (Pill Creek, moonlight), *1928. Oil and pencil on canvas, 49.6 x 59.8 cm*

(Lee's former mentor and lover), the poet Paul Eluard, British Surrealist Eileen Agar and, on a passing visit, Henry Moore. Agar recalled how Penrose was always 'ready to turn the slightest encounter into an orgy'. He and Miller photographed the fun from all

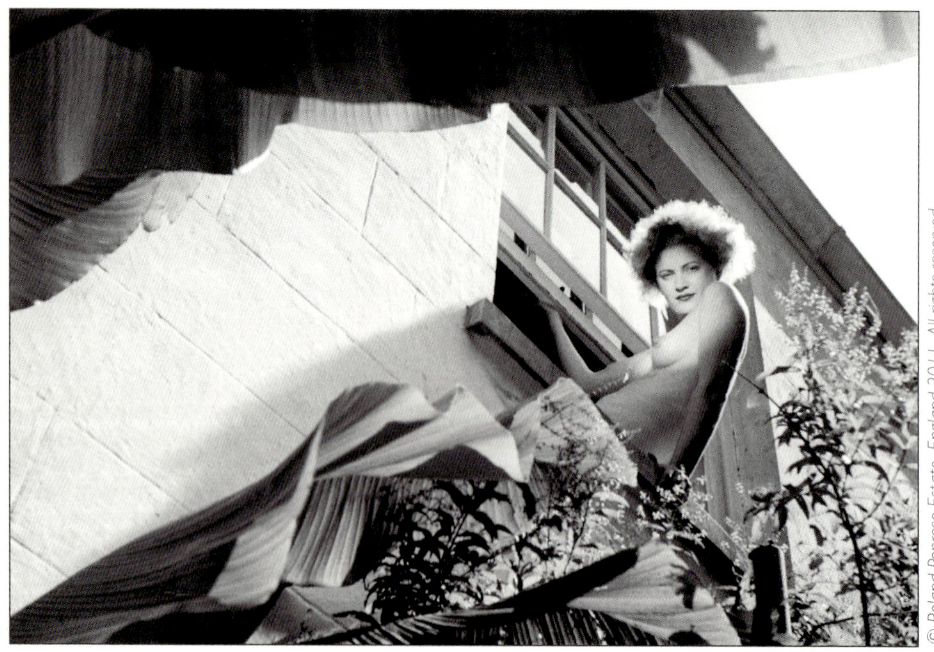

Roland Penrose, Lee Miller, hanging out of window, Lambe Creek, Cornwall, UK, 1937. *29.8 x 39.2 cm*

angles (above), and the whole group signed a 'wish you were here' postcard to their comrade Picasso, who was otherwise engaged in Paris, putting the finishing touches to his great protest painting *Guernica*.

During the week Penrose and his guests drove into the nearby port of Falmouth, where he bought an old ship's figurehead with bared breasts that reminded him of Lee – delighted, as Surrealists always were, in this junkshop discovery of an erotically charged object. The town's best-known artist, the prolific Henry Scott Tuke, had also specialized in nakedness, though of a less sexually forthright kind. Born in 1858, Tuke grew up in Falmouth, where his father was a doctor, and

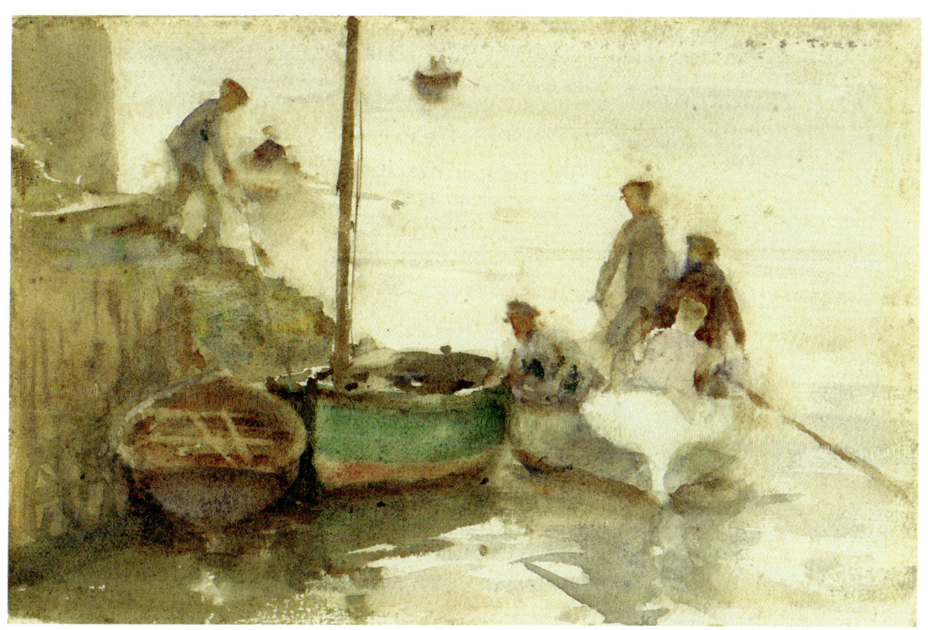

Henry Scott Tuke, At the Quay, *undated (c.1920?). Watercolour, 14 x 21.5 cm*

studied art in London and Paris before moving briefly to Newlyn. His work combines the sober realism of Newlyn painting with a more airy, Impressionist-style feel (above). Whereas Newlyn School paintings are usually populated by working-class women, children and old men, Tuke was celebrated for his scenes of adolescent boys, boating, swimming and sunbathing, often unselfconsciously naked. Perhaps young men's lives really were less harsh around Falmouth's boatyards, oyster beds and deep-water harbour with its ocean-going trade than in the struggling mines and fishing grounds towards Land's End.

Falmouth Estuary opens into a wide bay on the southernmost edge of which the Helford River flows in from the west. Among its branching creeks the grounds of large houses

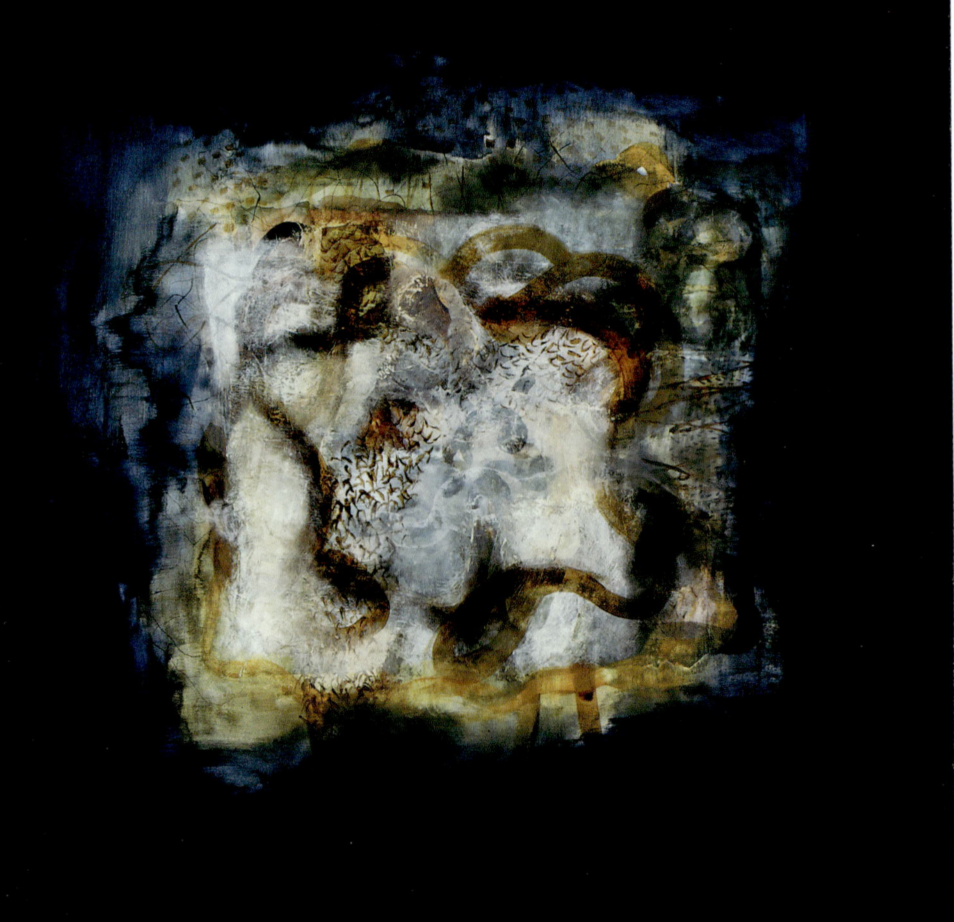

Louise McClary, Luminary Dusk, *2009. Mixed media on linen, 170 x 170 cm*

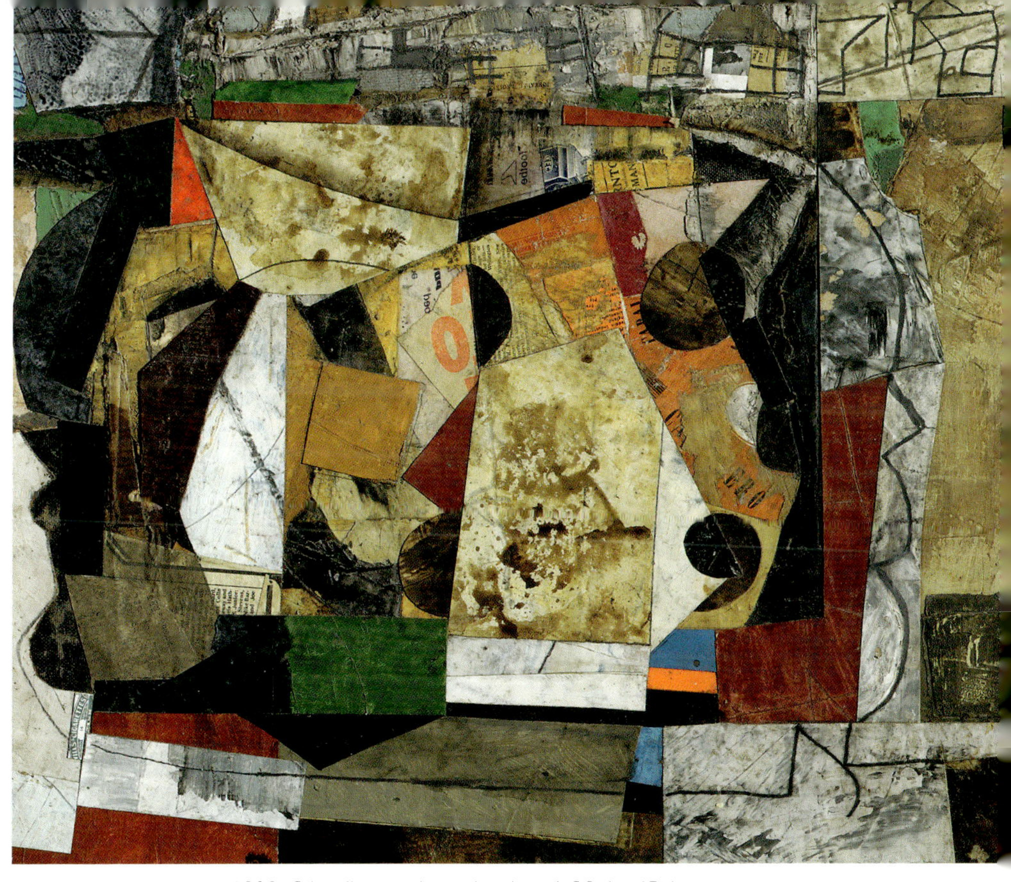

Bryan Ingham, Kynance, *1990. Oil, collage and pencil on board, 39.4 x 45.4 cm*

run down to the waterfront, 'shrouded by the trees, hidden from the eyes of men,' in Daphne du Maurier's phrase. This was the landscape of her home, Menabilly – the original of Manderley in her popular novel *Rebecca* – and the setting for another of her novels, *Frenchman's Creek*, in which a breathless historical romance takes place amid the

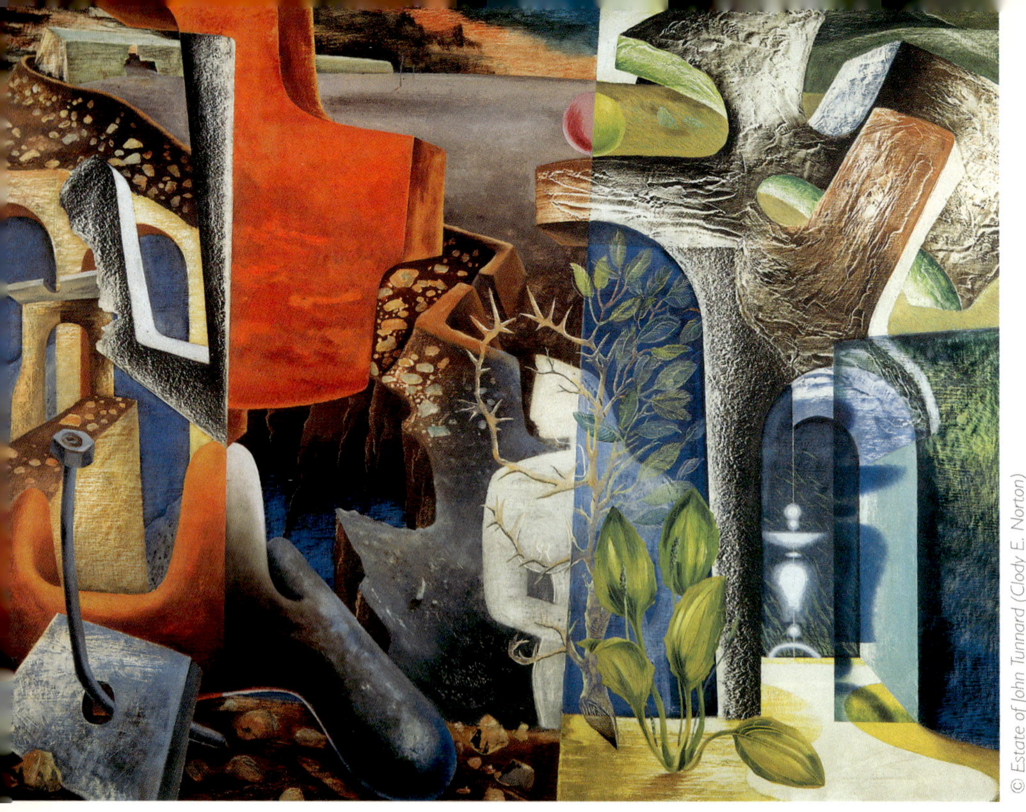

John Tunnard, Return*, 1951. Oil on gesso prepared canvas, laid on board, 114.3 x 152.4 cm*

drowsy, sensual atmosphere of summer on the Helford. Curiously, the heroine's lover, a recreational gentleman-pirate from Brittany, also is a serious amateur artist. In the Helford's upper reaches, towards Helston, dense oak woods run down to mudflats, which are carved at low tide with gleaming serpentine rivulets. It feels like another country again, not much visited and not much known in art. It's a landscape you find echoed in the abstract paintings of Louise McClary; in *Luminary Dusk* (2009), for example, the

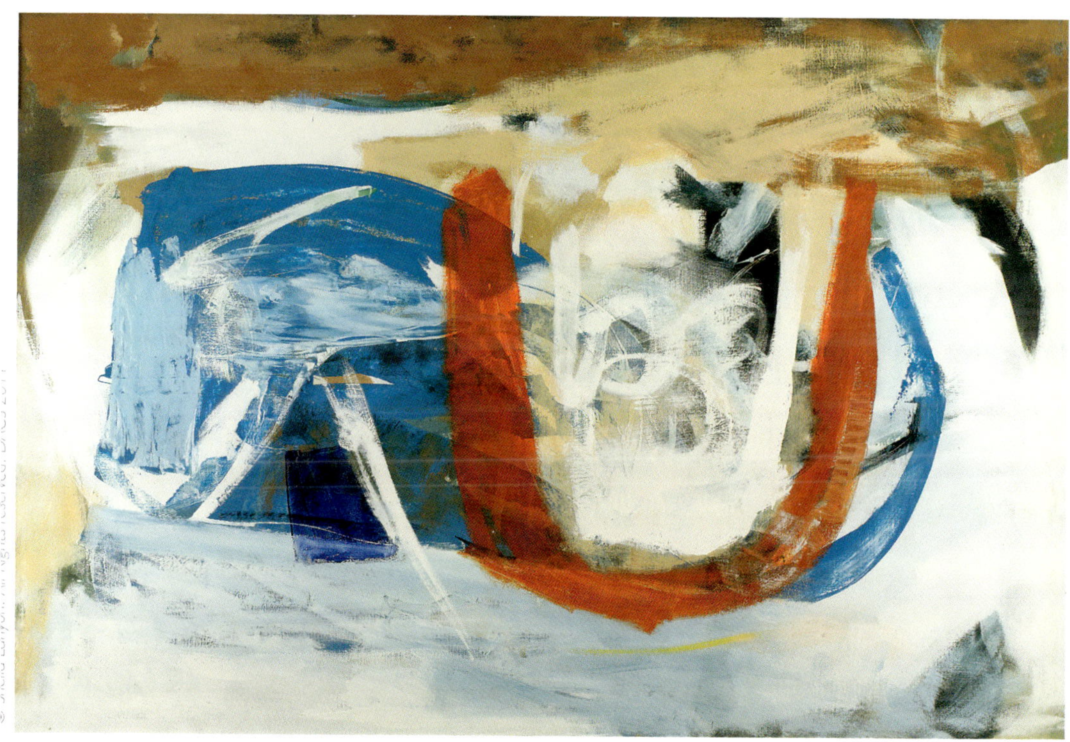

Peter Lanyon, Loe Bar, *1962. Oil on canvas, 122 x 183 cm*

intertwining shapes and lines suggest a map-like view of the woodland paths, but also the twisting oak boughs among which the river mists drift (page 46).

To the south of the Helford and Helston lies a short, blunt peninsula known as the Lizard (from the Cornish words for 'high place'). This is yet another of those micro-regions within Cornwall, like the china clay country or the Helford Estuary, where the geology, topography, flora and fauna have a self-contained distinctiveness. At the Helford end of the Lizard there's a naval air base, at the far tip (the furthest south you can get in Britain) a lighthouse. A succession of small coves and harbours rings the coast in between. Bryan Ingham's collage-painting *Kynance* (1990) takes its name from one of these coves (page 47). His method evokes the Cubist collages of Braque and Picasso, but it could also represent a beachcomber's eclectic haul, which in Cornwall often includes the mixed contents of recent wrecks and the sea-floor raked by storm tides. For much of the time between the early 1970s and his death in 1997 Ingham lived at Jollytown, an almost inaccessible homestead at the edge of the air base. 'Part chance, part choice,' he wrote, 'I found an old farmhouse by the sea, solid built with oil lamps at night and water from the well.' International modern art and remote granite hovels; what was it about this combination that proved so creatively productive for Ingham and for many of his contemporaries in Cornwall?

As early as 1933 John Tunnard, artist, jazz musician and former textile designer, had left London for a similarly isolated spot a few miles away at Cadgwith, on the Lizard's southernmost edge. Here he pursued a highly personal fusion of Surrealist and geometric abstract art (page 48). The dreamlike architectural structures in Tunnard's paintings are often anchored in a strong physical sense of the textures of sea and land. His expertise as a naturalist, and the close observation of the sea he developed through working as a coastguard during the Second World War, are balanced by his fascination with advanced technology and, from the 1950s, space exploration. It's the atmosphere rather than surfaces of this same landscape – its metamorphic drama of light and weather – that you find in Judy Buxton's work. In paintings such as *Carleon Cove (Autumn)* (page 52), though the landscape seems almost to dissolve in the vivid brushwork, you still get your bearings from the intuited contrast between earth, air and breaking waves.

You could think of this fascination with the meeting point of land and sea and sky as part of the way in which artists often seem drawn to what's going on at the edge of things, where other people tend not to look. This is true, in a different sense, of those irrepressible images of people going about their ordinary lives, closely observed as though for the pure pleasure of observation, in the margins of medieval manuscripts. Some of the oldest

Facing page: Breage Parish Church. St Christopher carries the Christ Child (L); Christ of the Trades (R)

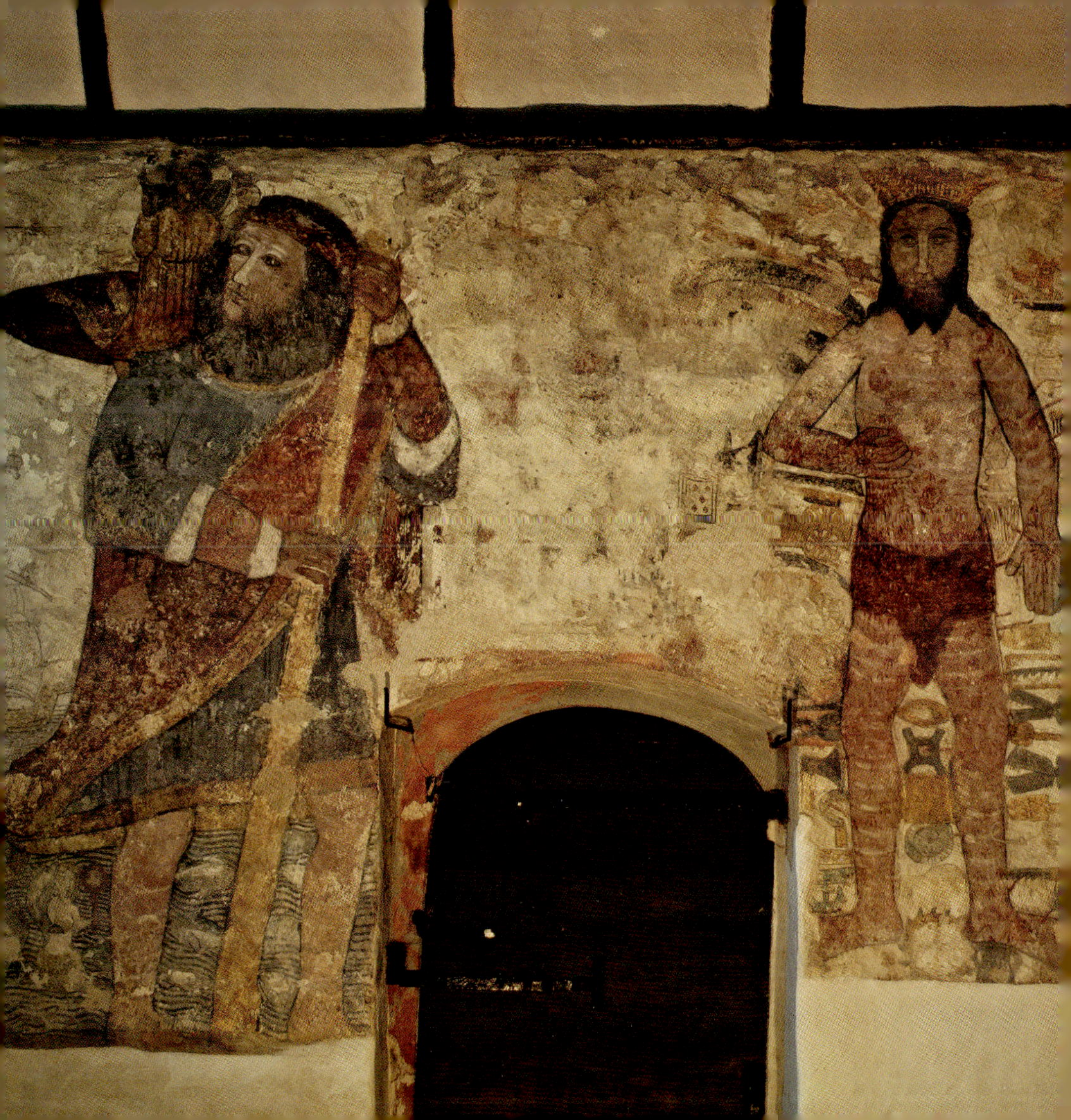

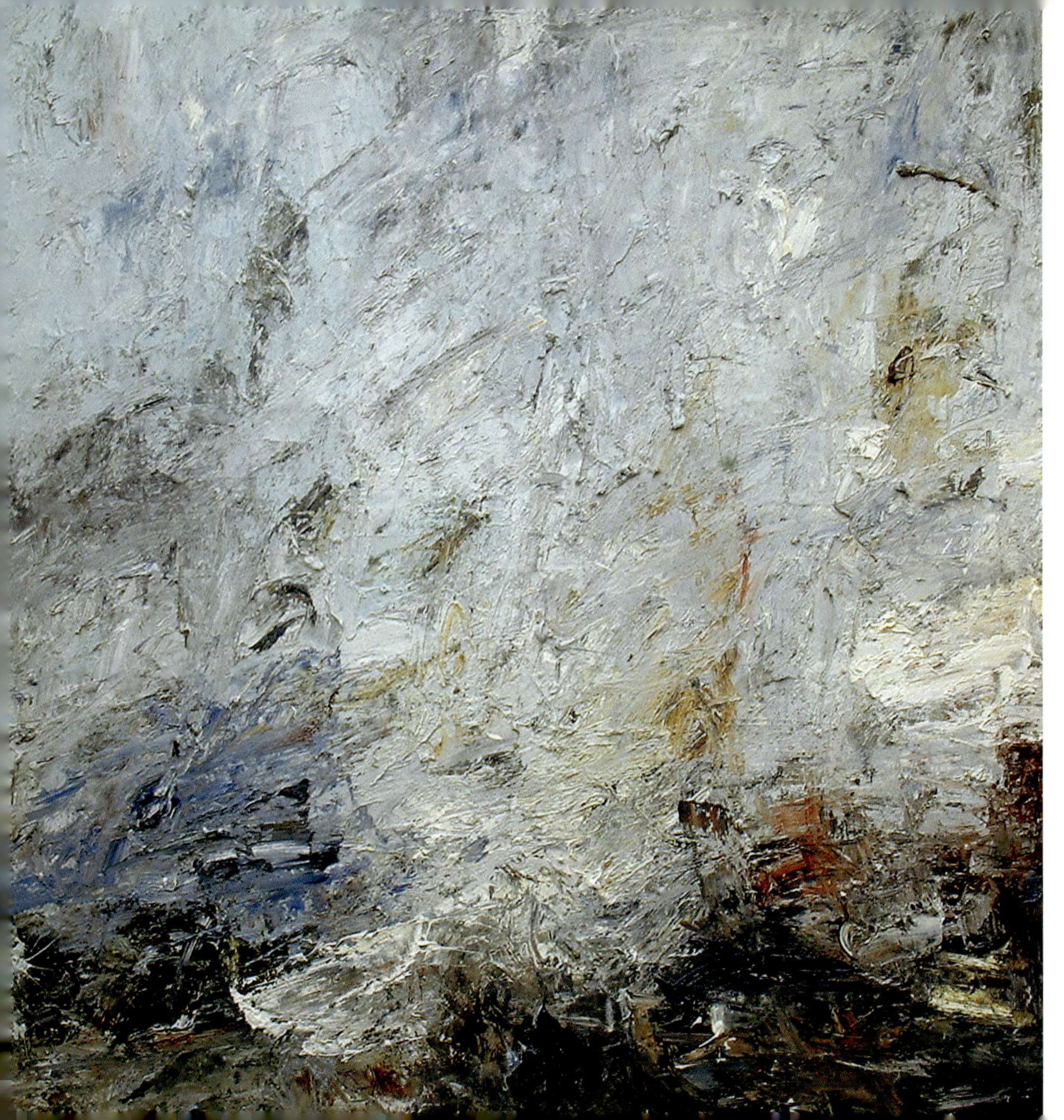

paintings in Cornwall belong to this medieval world, when the artist's task was to turn stories (usually Bible stories) into pictures, rather than to express their personal feelings or ideas. In the fifteenth-century parish church at Breage, off the main road between Helston and Penzance, wall paintings were uncovered in 1890 after having been hidden for centuries under layers of whitewash. They show two gigantic figures either side of a doorway in the church's north wall: on the left, St Christopher carries the Christ Child on his shoulders across a stream; on the right is a crowned figure known as Christ of the Trades (page 51). He stands in a kind of halo consisting of miniature hammers, spades, wagons – every kind of tool and product representing the trades that kept the wheels of medieval society turning.

There is something of the spirit of these two emblematic figures in Peter Lanyon's tall painting *Porthleven* (1951). Lanyon laboured for many months over this commission for the Festival of Britain, eventually (he said) destroying the original canvas and repainting the work rapidly in its final form. It takes its title from the harbour village of Porthleven, not far south of Helston and Breage. Its interlocking shapes echo the structure of a harbour seen from above, as well as the ground-level view of gantries, masts and fishing gear. After a few moments, two towering human figures also seem to materialize from *Porthleven*'s abstract-looking lines: a shawled woman on the right and on the left a man, lifting one arm aloft as though holding a miner's lamp. Lanyon said that these figures emerged unintentionally. They are ghosts of an earlier Cornwall to which his imagination constantly returned, where dark-clothed women worked on the quaysides and thousands of miners laboured underground. In 1959, Lanyon's quest for new angles on his native landscape led him to take up gliding. His painting *Loe Bar* (1962) is named for a sandbar near Porthleven but, in contrast to the earlier painting, it evokes the exhilaration of viewing a landscape from the air, amid the spiralling action of thermals and the moving clouds (page 49).

After passing between Breage and Porthleven, the road westwards soon reaches Marazion on the edge of Mount's Bay, where a tidal causeway tenuously links the pyramidal bulk of St Michael's Mount to the mainland. Before the gentlemen-artists colonized Newlyn and St Ives, the Mount

Facing page: Judy Buxton, Carleon Cove (Autumn)*, 2009. Oil on canvas, 91.4 x 96.5 cm*

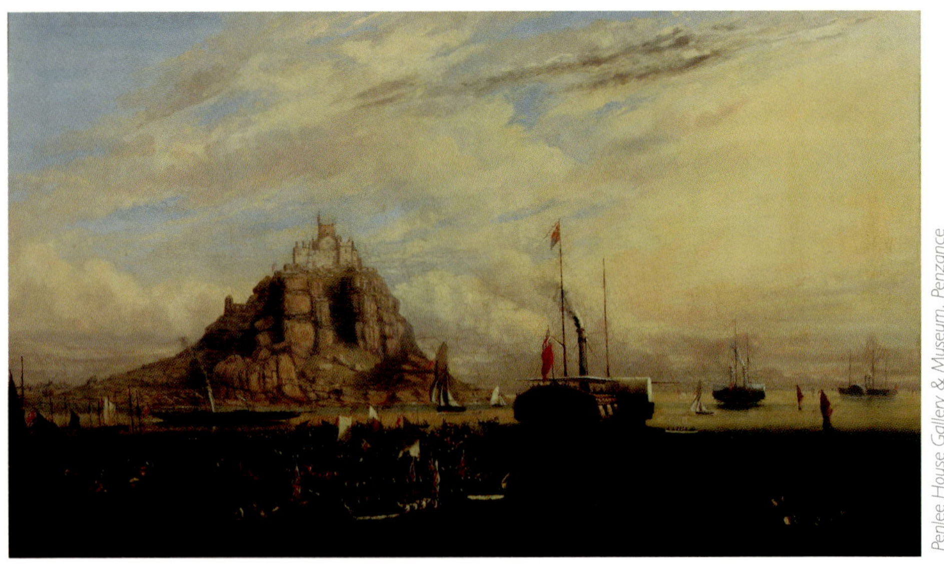

Penlee House Gallery & Museum, Penzance

John Grenfell Moyle, The Departure of Queen Victoria and Prince Albert from St. Michael's Mount, *1846. Oil on canvas, 76 x 129 cm*

was Cornwall's most famous topographical feature. It is mentioned by Milton in *Paradise Lost* and provides the setting for an extensive repertory of legends, involving a cast of mythical giants, the young Jesus and the archangel Michael, among others. Victorian painters loved its mixture of ruggedness and romance, which sets the tone for a painting by the local amateur Dr Moyle commemorating Queen Victoria and Prince Albert's visit to St Michael's Mount in September 1846 (above). Westwards, towards the roseate light of the evening sun and out of the frame of Moyle's vista, lie Penzance and Newlyn, linked by a seafront promenade along the facing curve of the bay (seen in Garstin's painting opposite).

Penzance and Newlyn to the Isles of Scilly

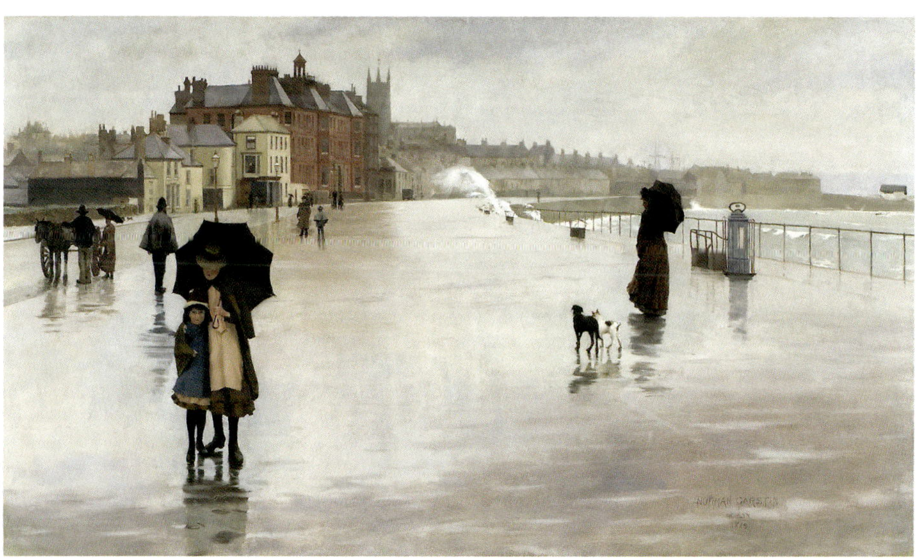

Norman Garstin, The Rain it Raineth Every Day, *1889. Oil on canvas, 94 x 162.5 cm*

In Penzance station – a granite barn of a place built in 1879 – the Great Western Railway reached its furthest limit. This is where Victorian artists, alighting with their *plein-air* painting kits, set off on the final leg of the long journey to Newlyn. They were entering the westernmost stub of Cornwall, an area known as West Penwith, which was to become home to one of the most densely settled and long-lived art colonies in history.

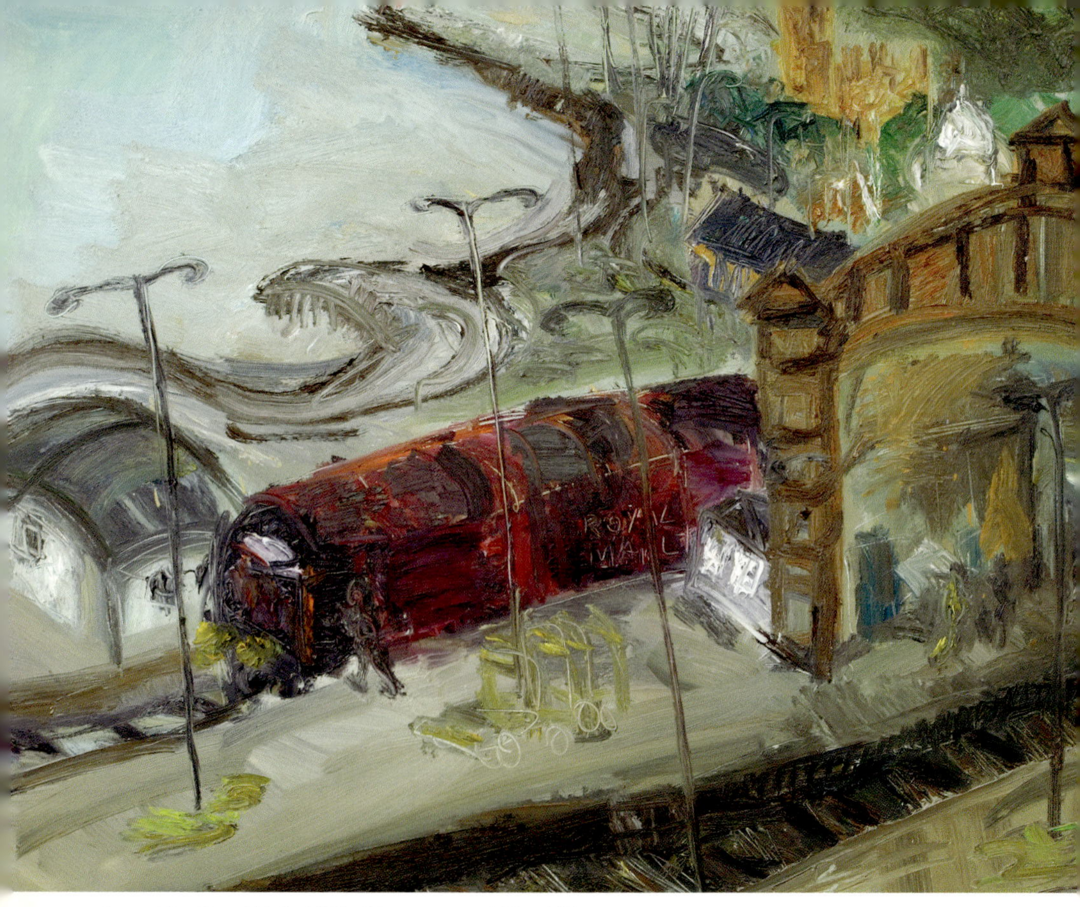

Partou Zia, Royal Mail, *1998. Oil on canvas, 102 x 127 cm*

The close proximity of so many artists in this small area, and their geographical distance from everywhere else, didn't always make for harmony. It could feel, observed Trevor Bell much later, as though you were 'living on an island at the bottom of a bucket'.

In Partou Zia's painting of Penzance Station (1998; page 56) almost every feature speaks of travels and transitions, such as the Iranian-born Zia experienced herself: the red mail train, the arched opening of the station hall, the arabesque of the advancing or receding tide just yards from the platform edge. The real voyaging, however, goes on in what Zia called 'the poetic zone', where the paths of memory cross the present moment.

No one talks about a 'Penzance School' of artists in the way they do about Newlyn and St Ives. Yet from the late nineteenth century onwards, many of the artists whose names are usually linked to Newlyn or St Ives actually lived and worked around Penzance. In 1853 it became the first town west of Bristol to get its own school of art – one of a spate of such institutions founded in the wake of the 1851 Great Exhibition with the aim of developing British artisans' skills in design. For the art colonists too, Penzance had its attractions. The town had prospered on maritime trade in the early 1800s; it offered more spacious, rather classier accommodation than was to be had in the cramped, working-class harbour villages along the coast.

In 1889, after brief forays into architecture and diamond-prospecting, the Irish painter Norman Garstin settled in Penzance. A large work he painted that same year, *The Rain It Raineth Every Day* (page 55), shows the town's storm-swept promenade in sullen weather. As a wave bursts against the sea wall, sending spray arching over the road, dark-clad figures shrink from the wind and wet. Garstin arranged these figures carefully, as though on a stage set. Although Garstin's Penzance is easily recognizable today, his seafront promenade has something of a Parisian boulevard about it. He had studied in Paris, where he would have seen Impressionist streetscapes, such as Paul Signac's *Boulevard Clichy in the Snow*, and the currently fashionable Japanese woodblock prints with their graphic dramas of daily life. His title, from a song Shakespeare used in *Twelfth Night* and again in *King Lear*, is a wry comment on Cornish winter weather but also a clue to the way Garstin deliberately highlighted the poetic and dramatic aspects of this scene of everyday Victorian provincial life.

For anyone growing up in west Cornwall in the early twentieth century who wanted to become an artist, Penzance School of Art was a more serious choice than the small private painting schools in St Ives and Newlyn, which tended to cater more for passing visitors. It was at Penzance that Peter Lanyon

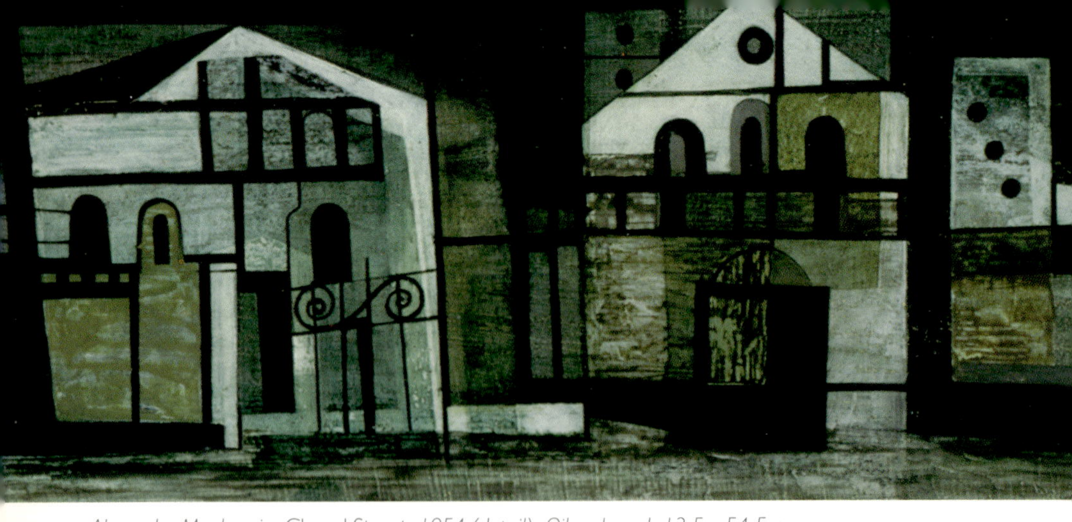

Alexander Mackenzie, Chapel Street, *1954 (detail). Oil on board, 12.5 x 54.5 cm*

began his training in 1936 and later, along with John Wells and Denis Mitchell, learned printmaking, and where John Tunnard taught for twenty years from 1945. Alexander Mackenzie was one of the new wave of young artists who congregated in west Cornwall after the Second World War. What drew him down from Liverpool in 1951 was a teaching job in a Penzance school, rather than the lure of an artistic community, but he was soon attracted to the work of John Wells, now installed in a former studio of Stanhope Forbes's in Newlyn, and Ben Nicholson. Mackenzie adopted their practice of painting on wooden panels, which could be scraped down to reveal layers of colour, glowing with translucent delicacy as the white ground showed through. In *Chapel Street* (1954; above), he articulated the granite and brick façades of this historic Penzance street to form interconnected semi-abstract patterns. Mackenzie saw parallels between painting and archaeology: when you explore the layers of an archaeological site, he explained, you see signs of what has happened there, but you can never be sure. Such places have

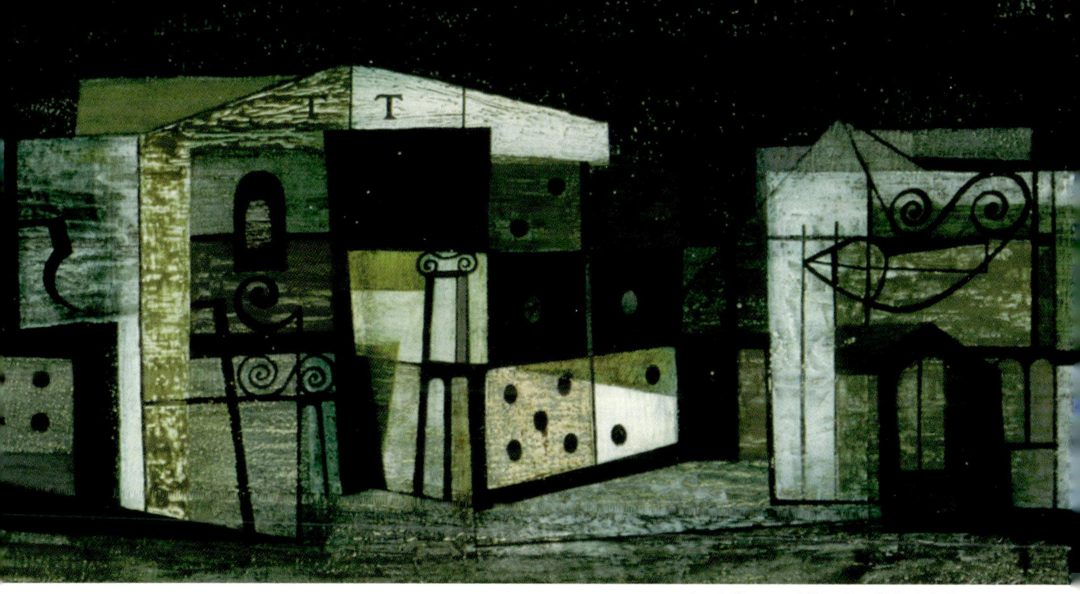

'a certain amount of mystery' – just as 'there should be with painting, I think'.

Chapel Street runs down past St Mary's Church (visible in Garstin's *The Rain It Raineth*) to Penzance harbour, one of the sources that Anthony Frost taps for material – quite literally – for his paintings. In *The Colour of Sound* (2008), the eyelet in a piece of sail can be seen top right (page 60). Frost uses ripstop (synthetic sailcloth), jagged strips of scrim and canvas, rope or supermarket netting to create intensely coloured collage-paintings. The stretched marine textiles contribute to a sense in which oceanic blues or football-strip reds are pulled into taut harmony, as a sail tightens with the wind.

A mile or so inland along this south-facing coast, squeezed in between the ports and the Penwith moors, the local mine-owners and landed gentry made space for their country mansions and gardens, stocked with exotic species that flourished in the mild Gulf Stream climate after finding their way to Cornwall in ships' cargoes or being captured on plant-hunting expeditions. At Trengwainton on the outskirts of Penzance, tree ferns,

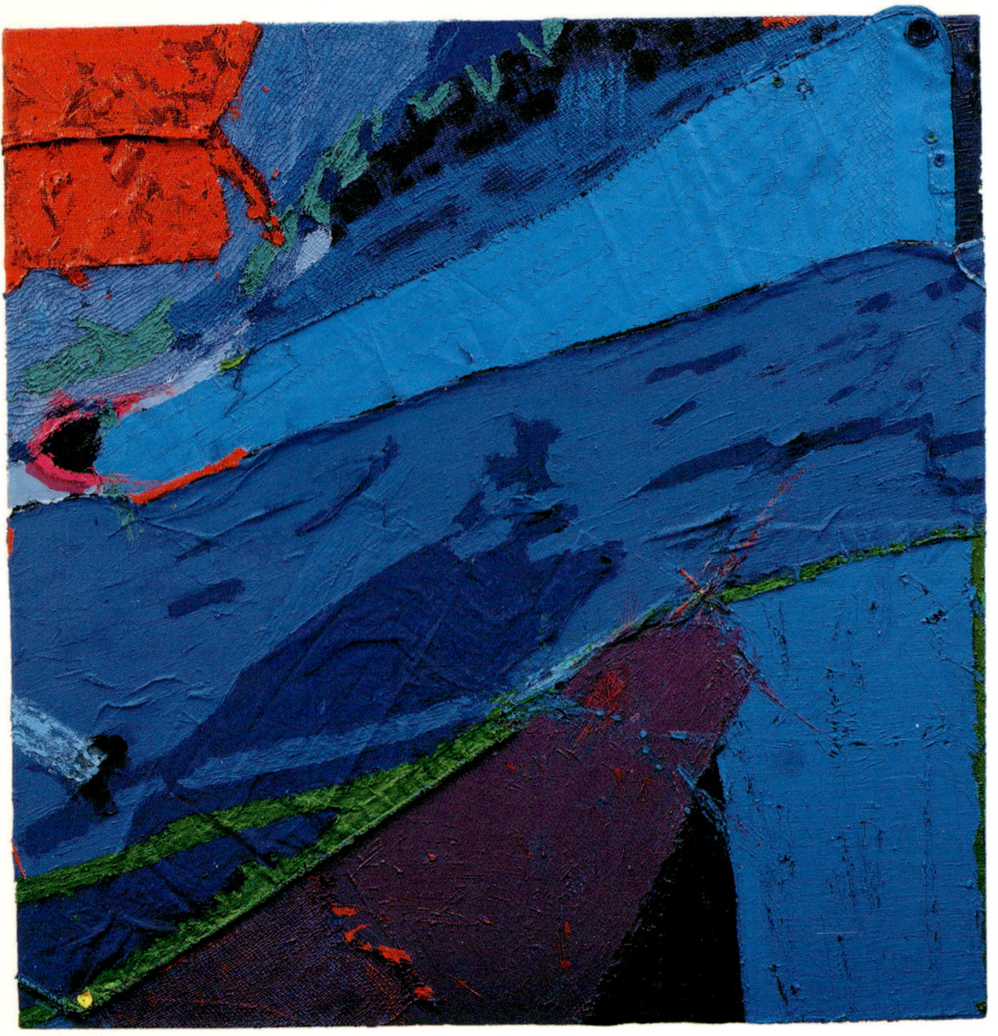

camellias and huge magnolias populate what was once just a stream valley. In its sense of flowing movement, Felicity Mara's painting *The Bridge (Twilight)* (2007; page 63) takes its cue from this quiet, concealed landscape of trees and water. The sinuous calligraphic brushstrokes evoke the experience of watching and listening to the stream as it flows beneath a narrow wooden bridge.

When Terry Frost returned to live in Cornwall in 1974, he chose Newlyn rather than his old haunt of St Ives, which he felt (even then) had been overrun by tourism. He may have been influenced by his friend and artistic sparring partner Roger Hilton's earlier association with Newlyn, where he rented a studio from the harbourmaster in the 1950s. Hilton was never a landscape artist, but boat shapes crept into his abstract paintings, such as *The Blue Boat* (c.1957–8; page 64). His wife, Rose, recalled how the harbourmaster used the paintings Hilton gave him to repair the studio after he left. Here's Frost's account of starting the day in his own studio high above Newlyn, overlooking Mount's Bay:

Facing page: Anthony Frost, The Colour of Sound, *2008. Acrylic and pumice on netting, hessian scrim, sail, sacking hessian, Post Office bag and canvas, 190.5 x 190.5 cm*

> The sun comes up over the Lizard in the morning. St Michael's Mount starts off like a Japanese woodcut, a triangle of island and castle nudging through a shroud of mist, and then to the right is a red glow, and if you wait and watch the sun comes up, first as a semi-circle and then a circle behind the Mount, there is a red reflection shimmering in the water, and that's my morning treat.

You can visualize exactly what he's describing, a scene he says he photographed a hundred times, but you're also invited to see it as an abstract painting, 'a semi-circle and then a circle'. The delight in natural phenomena and the excitement in abstract art often come so close in Frost's work that you can't tell one from the other. Strongly defined shapes and extrovert colour characterize even his latest paintings, such as *Frisky* (page 65), made shortly before his death in 2003. We're a long way from the muted tones and serious subjects favoured by Victorian painters in the harbourside streets down below Frost's studio. Here in 1888 Stanhope Forbes painted *The Village Philharmonic*; this heartwarming scene, in which a motley amateur ensemble practises in a Newlyn loft, won him a Gold Medal at the Paris Salon. In the same year,

Forbes's ruefully unsuccessful contemporary Vincent van Gogh was in Arles painting his *Night Café*. Like *The Village Philharmonic*, it is set in a provincial interior organized around the long inclined plane of a table. Where Forbes's room is all shadowy browns and greys, however, Van Gogh's is a vivid nocturnal bloom of red, yellow and green. He wanted to create a kind of 'colour music' that is, in fact, much closer to Frost's preoccupations than the work of early Newlyn artists.

An engaging feature of nineteenth-century Newlyn School paintings is the artists' understated but evidently genuine affection for their adopted home and its inhabitants. Walter Langley, who trained as a lithographer in Birmingham, was renowned for his scenes of village drama, such as the moment when women waiting anxiously on the quayside learn that their menfolk have been lost at sea. *The Sunny South* (page 66), in which an elderly farmworker rests on his shovel, strikes a note of quieter pathos. It's the kind of scene associated with the French painter of peasant life Jean-François Millet. Yet where Millet captured the bleakness and exhaustion of day-long labour in the fields, Langley's painting conveys the warmth of a spring day on the slopes above Newlyn, with the apple blossom bursting, the high sun warming the recently turned soil in the vegetable patch, and the distant sea a deep, alluring blue.

There's a similarly beguiling warmth in the low afternoon sunlight that patterns the classroom floor in Elizabeth Forbes's *School is Out* (page 67). This image of village children in smocks and hats could so easily be a sentimental set piece, if you didn't feel the artist's empathy with her subject so strongly. It is as though the place itself has benignly shaped the lives of the people who live there. This can't have been the whole truth; the artists, after all, were looking at Newlyn with the freedom of people who can come and go when they choose. But Elizabeth Forbes's observation of children is grounded in reality as well as being coloured by the popular nostalgia for childhood innocence.

The sixteen-year-old daughter of a Newlyn fisherman was the model for Dod Procter's painting *Morning*, which shot the young Cornish artist to fame after being voted 'Picture of the Year' at the Royal Academy in 1927 and subsequently purchased for the Tate Gallery. Hailed as 'a new vision of the human figure', it shows the girl reclining dreamily as the light pearls her pale

Facing: Felicity Mara, The Bridge (Twilight), *2007. Acrylic and charcoal on raw linen, 172 x 172 cm*

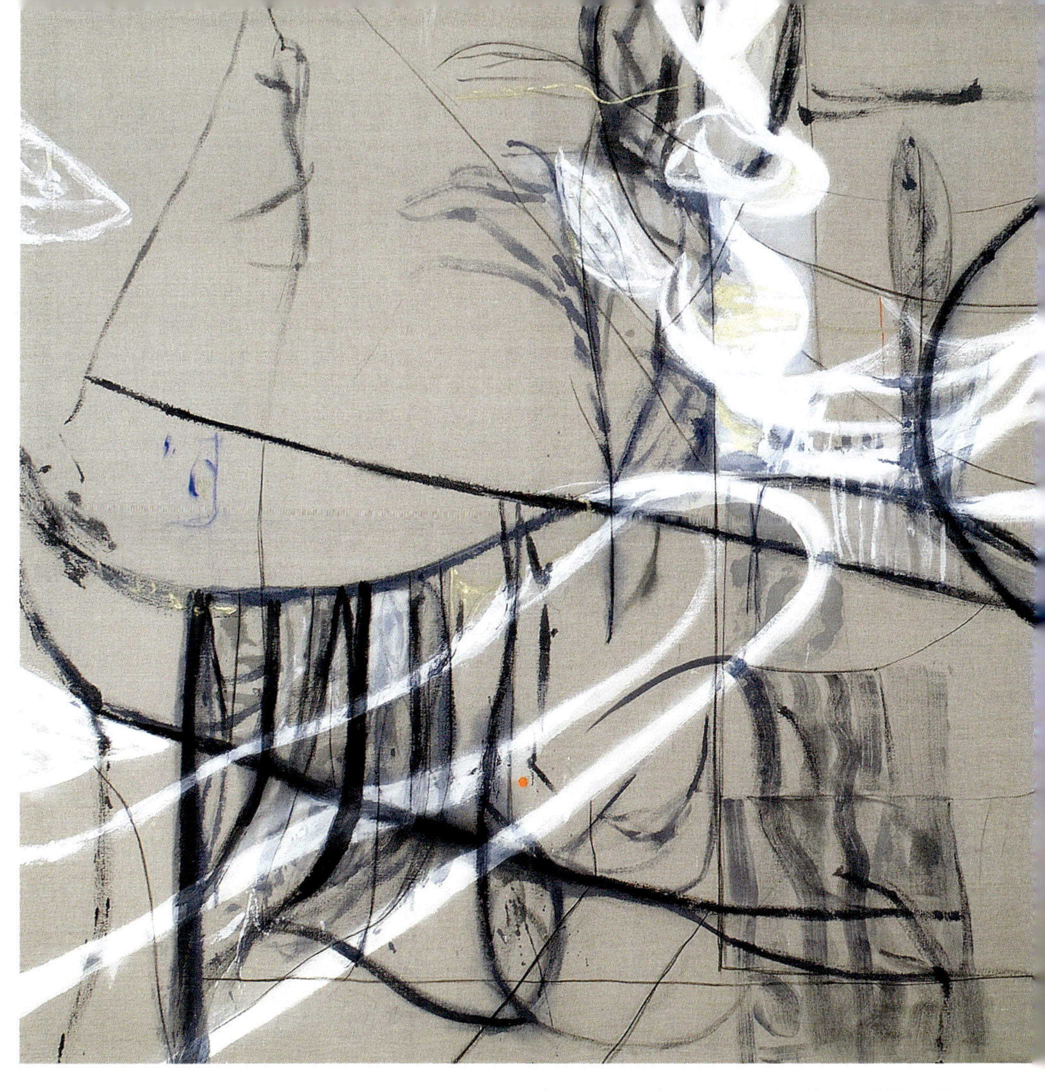

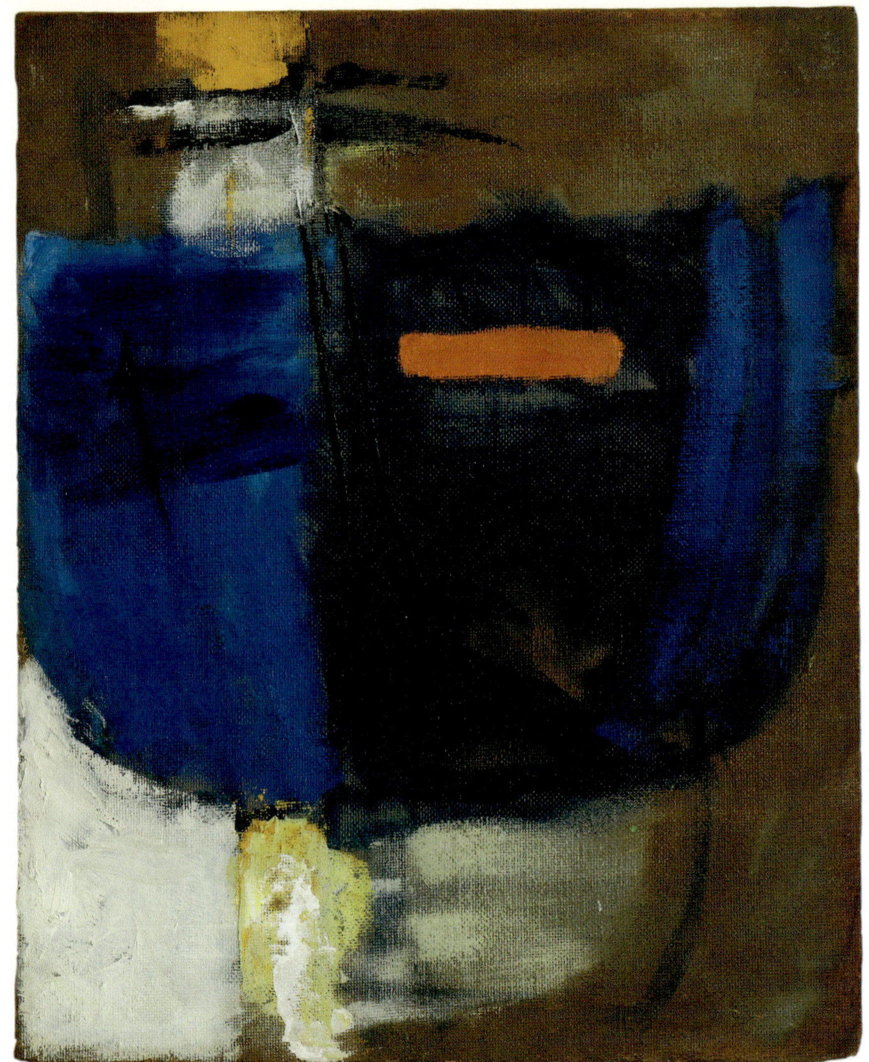

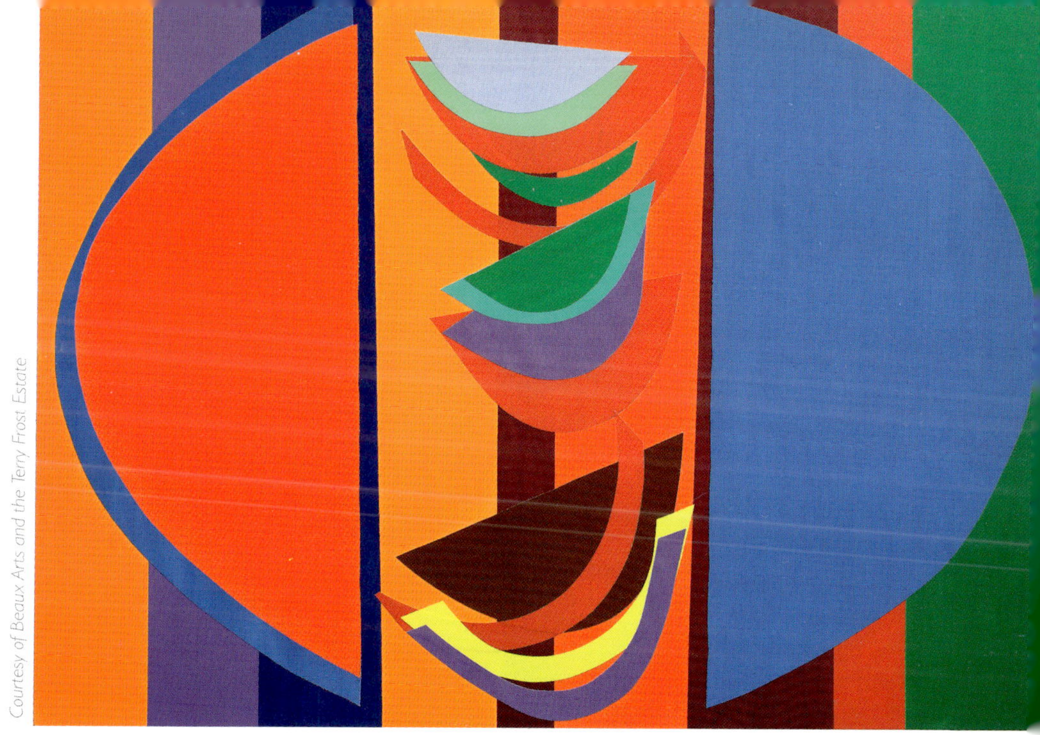

Terry Frost, Frisky, 2003. Acrylic and collage on canvas, 147 x 203 cm

shift and bedclothes. Procter studied at the Forbes's painting school, followed by a spell in Paris, and in 1942 was among the first female Royal Academicians to be elected. Her *Early Morning, Newlyn* (1926) is a view over the village in the same soft but defining sea-light (from its angle, a winter sunrise), with a hint of the Cubist geometries she must have encountered in Paris.

Facing page: Roger Hilton, Blue Boat, *c.1957–8. Oil on board, 61 x 50.8 cm*

In the work of Laura Knight, who arrived in Newlyn with her husband Harold in 1907, via the Yorkshire coastal art colony at Staithes, the brown tones of classic Newlyn School

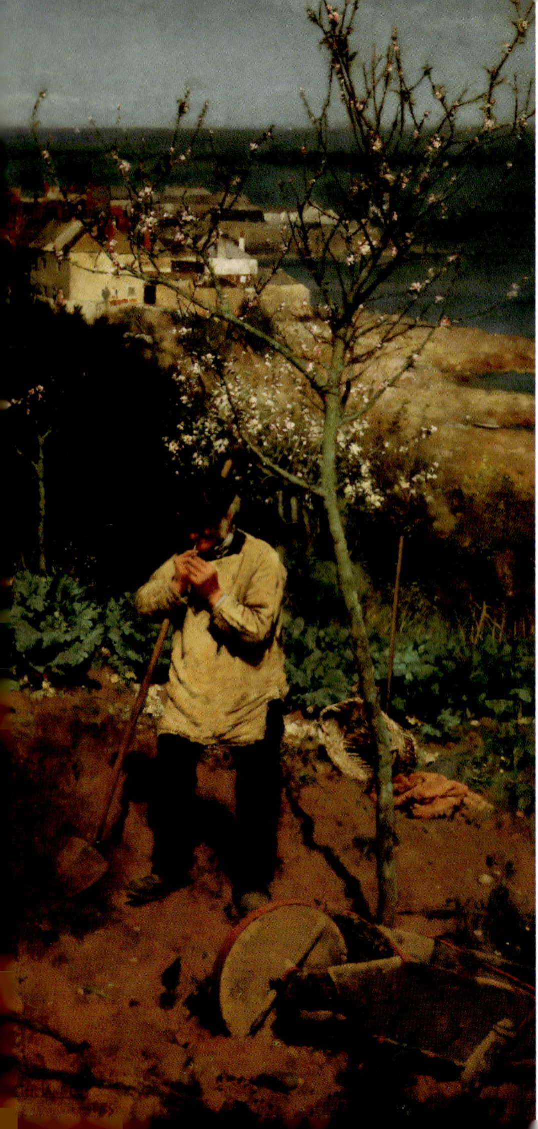

painting were replaced by livelier colours. Instead of working-class subject matter, she focused on a more stylish, prosperous world of leisure, in which girls with suntanned limbs in blazing white dresses lounge around near the sea's edge. Knight, Procter and other artists between the two world wars transformed this area of Cornwall (or at least its image in art) from a place of cloudy skies and worthy toil to a land touched by Mediterranean radiance. This was the British Riviera, a rival to the south of France where artists and tourists congregated in search of sunlight and colour – still a little on the wild side, but not too wild for comfort.

In the years after 1945, however, artists could hardly return with such conviction to evocations of timeless quiet and calm. Like many of his generation, William Scott spent several years in the army before he was free to paint again. From 1946 he painted for several summers in the tiny port of Mousehole (pronounced Mowsel), just beyond Newlyn. Scott wasn't interested in conventional landscape subjects. 'I don't respond much to air and sea and the things of nature,' he admitted.

Walter Langley, The Sunny South, 1885.
Oil on canvas, 122 x 61 cm

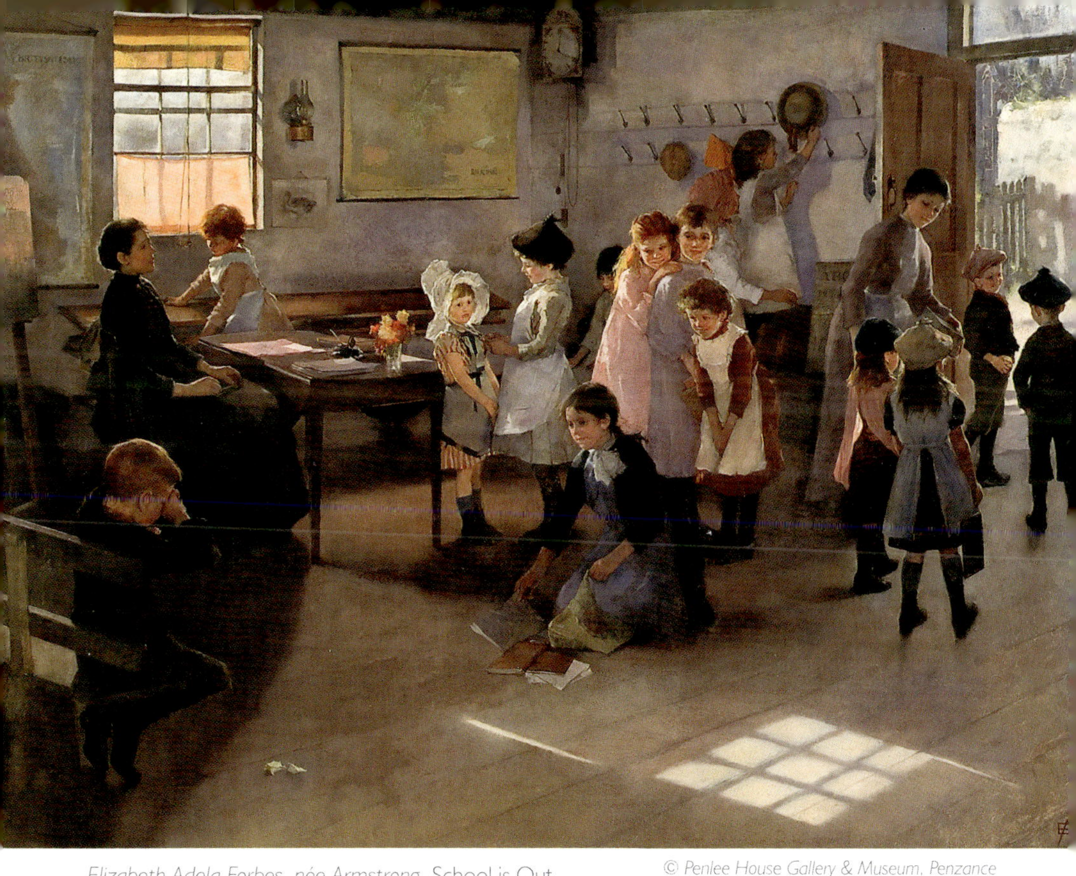

Elizabeth Adela Forbes, née Armstrong, School is Out, *1889. Oil on Canvas. 105 x 119 cm*

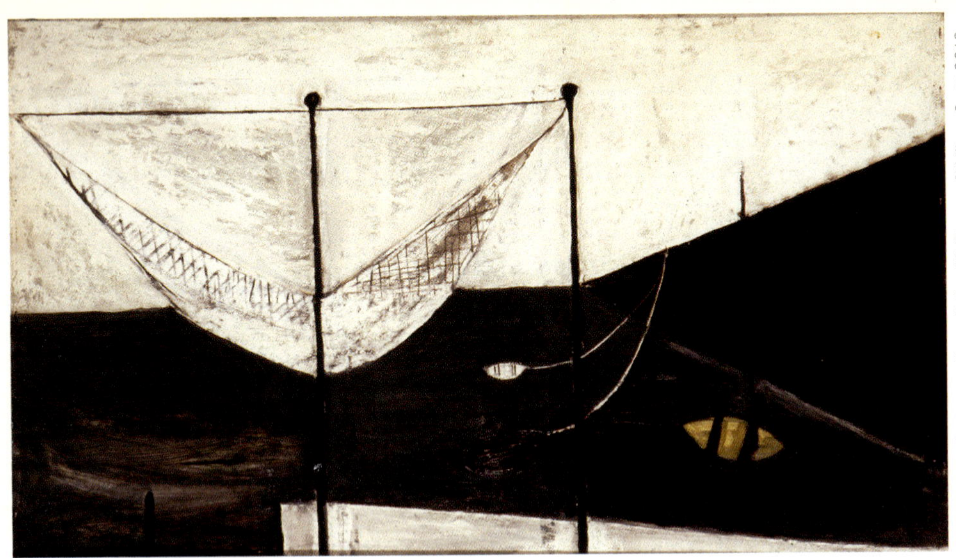

William Scott, Harbour, *1950 or 1951. Oil on board, 57.2 x 99.1 cm*

'When I approached landscapes it was the man-made thing that attracted me.' In *Harbour* (above), the shapes of outspread drying nets, boats and the harbour walls are recognizable but formalized to the point where they almost cross the border into complete abstraction. Above the harbour entrance was a large crane with a distinctive criss-cross arms, which appears repeatedly in modern paintings. You can see it at middle-left in Ben Nicholson's *November 11, 1947 (Mousehole)* (page 69), which brings together two aspects of Nicholson's work: his elegantly linear Cornish landscapes and his much more geometric and abstract still-lifes. It occurs too in work by the Mousehole-born artist Jack Pender. Rather than turning familiar features of the local landscape into semi-abstract forms, Pender used the structure and balance learned from abstract art to interpret his home territory and family history in the fishing community.

One of Pender's teachers at the West of England School of Art in Bristol was Paul Feiler. After a successful London show in 1953, Feiler bought an old Methodist chapel at

Ben Nicholson, November 11, 1947 (Mousehole), *1947. Oil and pencil on canvas mounted on wood, 46.5 x 58.5 cm*

Kerris, inland between Newlyn and Mousehole, where he later settled. The title of Feiler's *Boats and Sea* (page 70) sounds very literal, like a traditional marine painting. In fact, it is constructed from abstract shapes, built up with clearly defined brushmarks. The

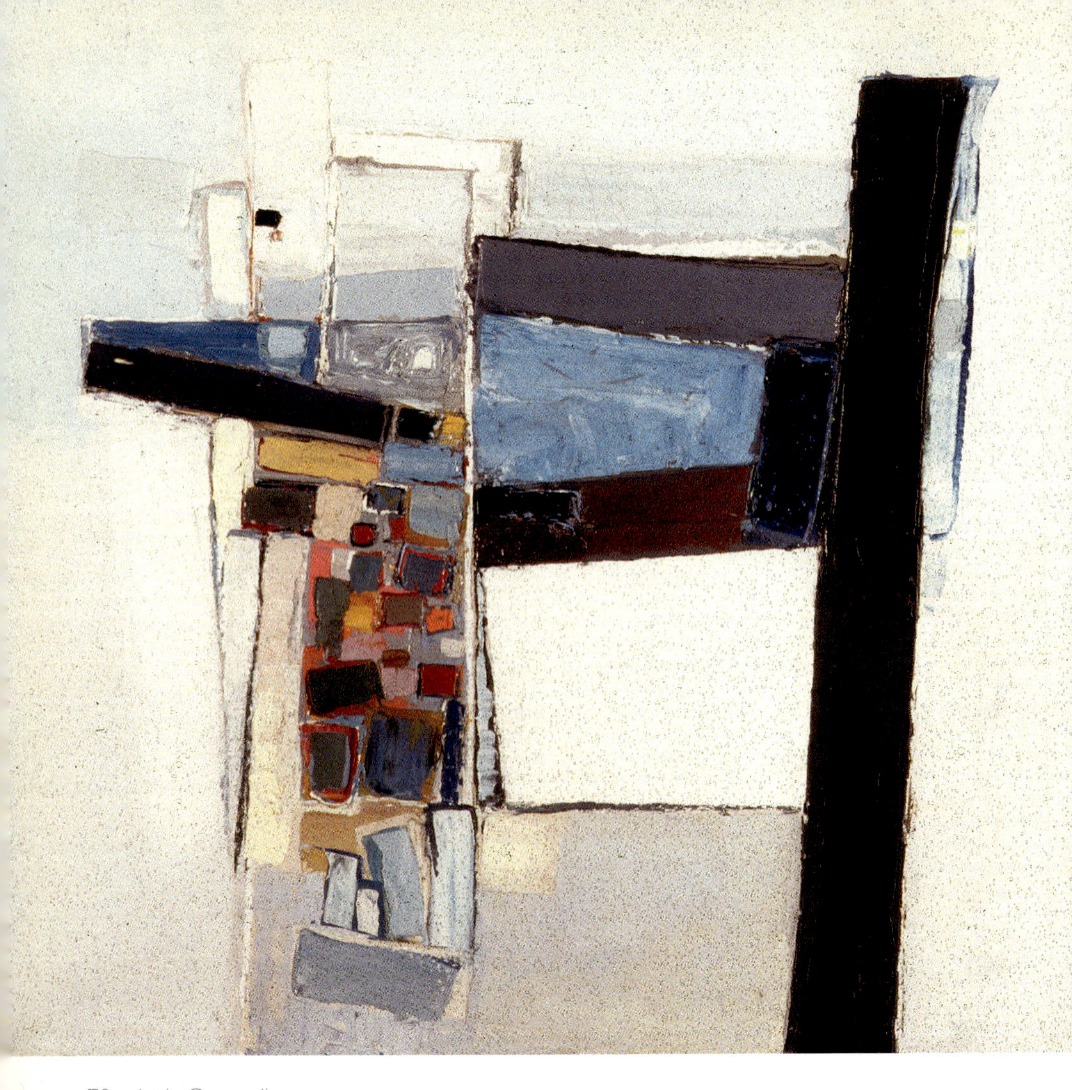

blues and greys are both the colours of painted boats and the changing colours of the sea, as though these could not be separated from each other. Feiler described his approach in terms of words as well as images: 'I have always enjoyed writing down with paint what I felt the world around me looked like.'

Mousehole is the last harbour village of any size on Cornwall's south coast. It's followed by a series of coves, backed by narrow, wooded valleys and separated by cliffs that get sheerer and grander towards Land's End. In the early twentieth century the Lamorna Valley, beyond Mousehole, was the epicentre of a group of artists, an offshoot of the original Newlyn School, whose members included Samuel John Birch and Laura Knight. Birch identified so strongly with the place that he adopted the name Lamorna (also to avoid confusion with fellow artist Lionel Birch). Though their landscapes look sturdy beside the iridescent effects of Monet or Renoir, the Lamorna painters were more indebted to Impressionism than their predecessors, emphasizing the play of sunlight on trees, rocks, sand and water. This is the atmosphere evoked by Knight's enormous portrait

Facing page: Paul Feiler, Boats and Sea, *1953. Oil on canvas, 87.5 x 90.8 cm*

of Birch and his two daughters (1913–34; page 72), a lyrical tribute to friendship, family and a shared love of place. Holding a daughter under one arm, grasping a tree with his other hand, and sporting a bow tie and briar pipe, Birch is a man of artistic property, in firm possession of the qualities of freshness and innocence that drew him to Lamorna.

Birch's *Morning Fills the Bowl* (page 73) takes a high-angle view between cliffs to the west of Lamorna Cove down into the small harbour from which granite from the nearby quarry was shipped (to build the Thames Embankment, among other structures). He gives a monumental presence to the natural forms; the shadow-side of the cliffs framing the sea's morning brilliance recall the epic scale of nineteenth-century paintings of the American Midwest. But this is no uninhabited Eden: the gantry on the pier and the mounds of broken quarry-stone reveal the presence of industry. You can't tell whether the viewer is meant to be turning back for a last glimpse of human activity before setting off into the wilds or gratefully arriving into sunlight from the darker, less hospitable side of nature. Like Stanhope Forbes, Laura Knight, Dod Procter and other Newlyn artists, Birch eventually became a Royal Academician; for a while Alfred Munnings, President of the Royal

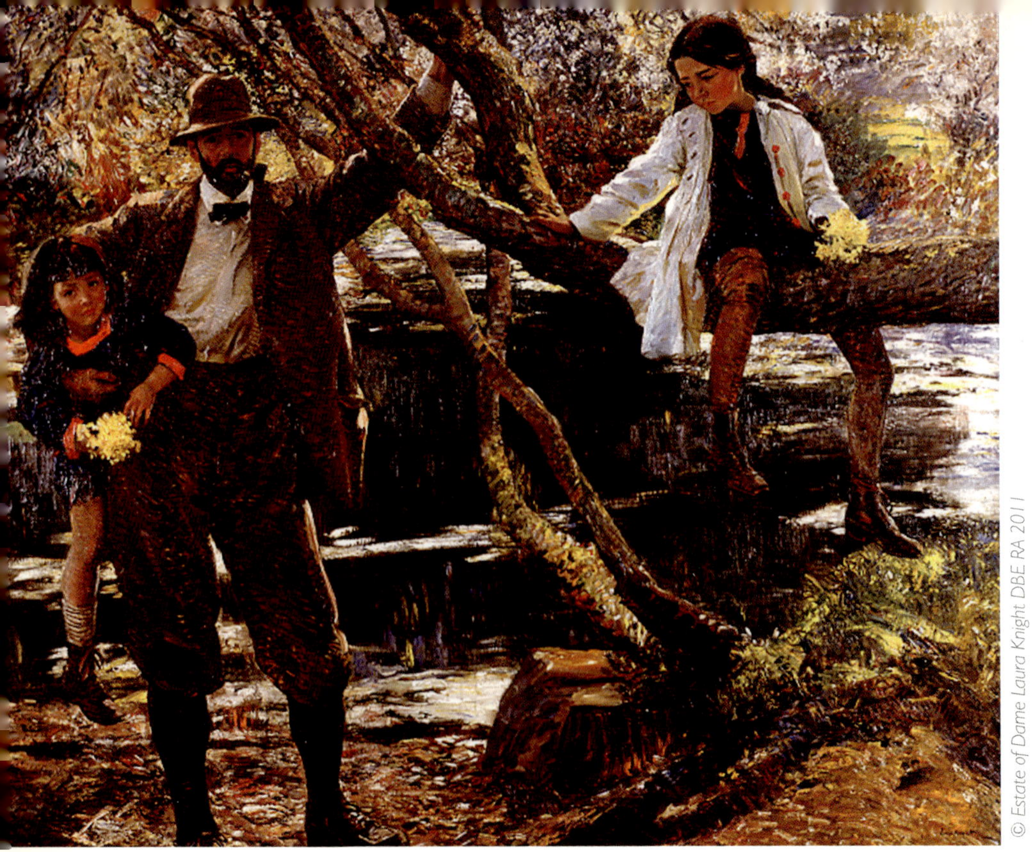

Laura Knight, 1877–1970, Lamorna Birch and His Daughters, *1933. Oil on canvas, 215 x 261 cm*

Academy and noted painter of horses and generals, was also part of the Lamorna group.

It was at Lamorna Cove too that the occultist, artist and writer Ithell Colquhoun lived from the 1940s until her death in 1988. Where Birch had seen around him a landscape of glowing wholesomeness, Colquhoun found a mysterious pagan world inhabited by 'nature-spirits weeping, imprisoned and misused by Druidism in decay'.

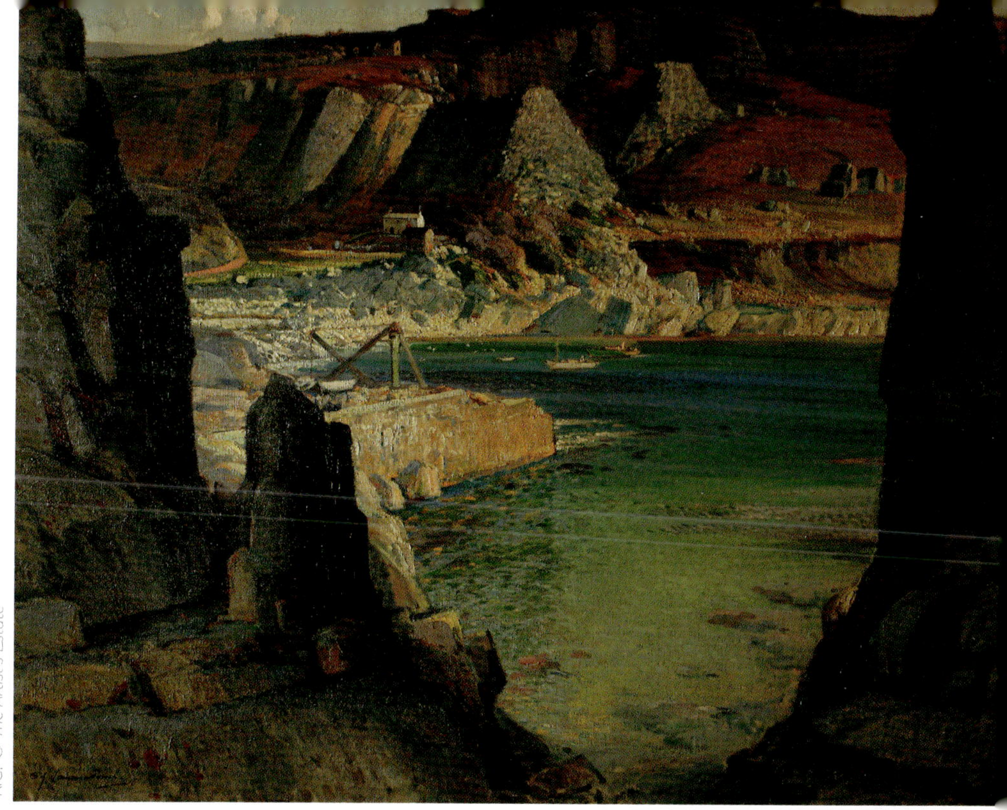

Samuel John (Lamorna) Birch, Morning Fills the Bowl, *1926. Oil on canvas, 114.5 x 145 cm*

In the 1930s she was involved with the Surrealist movement in Paris and London, and saw nature through Surrealist eyes, in erotic, dreamlike terms. Colquhoun's *Scylla* (a reference to the myth of Odysseus) shows twinned rocks rearing from a transparent coastal pool – suggested, she said, by the sight of her own raised legs in the bath. The sharp prow of a kayak just visible beyond the rocks (or legs), and the pubic fronds of seaweed curling between them, transform exploring rockpools into a metaphor for sex.

An older contemporary of Colquhoun's, and an equally unlikely inhabitant of the Lamorna Valley, was Marlow Moss. She studied sculpture, and later architecture, at Penzance School of Art and also worked in Paris, where she was taught by the Cubist painter Fernand Léger. Moss's type of modern art was quite different from Surrealism: it was based on pure geometric forms, which she used in paintings, sculptures and reliefs. Whereas Colquhoun had fallen under Dalí's spell, Moss admired Mondrian's austere abstract paintings (he was also said to have admired hers); her sculptures sometimes resemble three-dimensional realizations of Mondrian's ideas.

On his visit in 1811 Turner had been quick to see that the cliffs of Land's End and the savage reefs beneath had a quintessentially Romantic quality known as 'the Sublime' – the aspect of nature that inspired fear and wonder. Later, as tourism to Cornwall developed, Land's End became a place you had to visit simply because of what it represented – the county's westernmost extremity (being 'the last' of anything – England, Mohicans, whatever it might be – was also very Romantic). When photographer Lee Miller visited Cornwall with her Surrealist friends in July 1937, they duly made the pilgrimage to Land's End, and to Wolf Rock lighthouse beyond. In Miller's photograph of the lighthouse lantern, the multiple reflections look like the soundwaves of an echo, as though the light were discovering itself in a trance, Surrealist-style.

This isn't quite the end of the westward journey, though. Some 30 miles off Land's End lie the Isles of Scilly, once joined to the mainland but now barely above sea level. During the Second World War John Wells was the resident doctor on Scilly. Between looking after the islands' scattered population and helping to set up a general hospital on the largest island, St Mary's, he found time to paint and to plan his change of career from medicine to art. As a young man Wells had met the Nicholsons and Kit Wood on their trip to Cornwall in 1928. In the 1930s he stayed in touch with Ben Nicholson, who encouraged Wells to pursue his artistic vocation. As with other artists, his wartime work was necessarily small-scale and made from cheap materials, but this didn't prevent it expressing ideas that were shared by progressive European modern artists. A small drawing from 1942, *Untitled* (page 76), has clear affinities with the work that Nicholson,

Facing: Lee Miller, Lens of Land's End Lighthouse, Cornwall, UK, 1937. *Photograph, 38.4 x 29.9 cm*

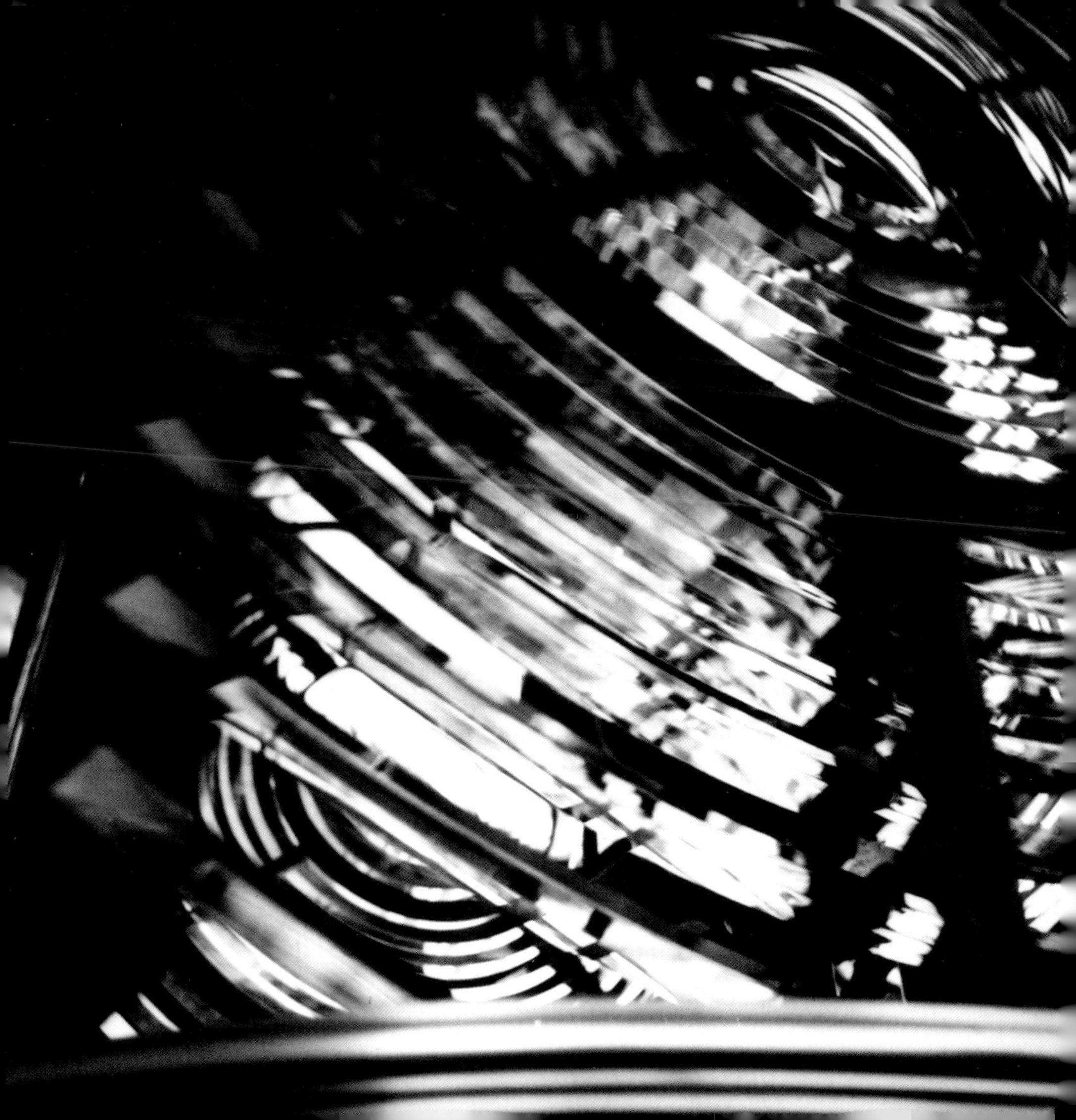

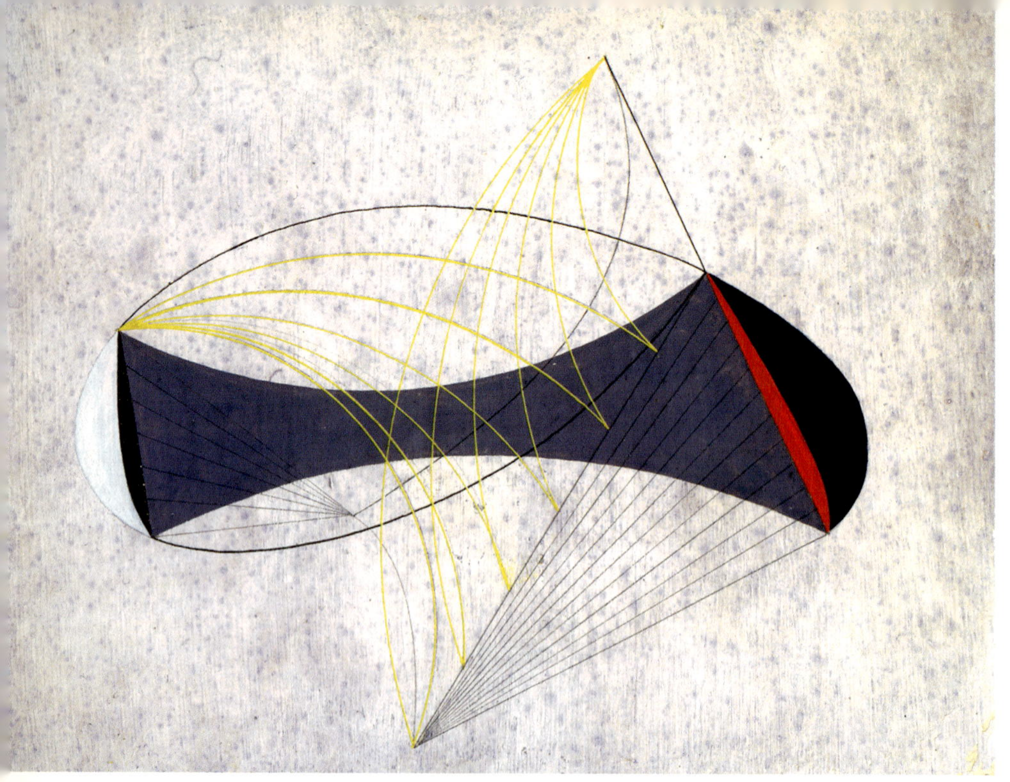

John Wells, Untitled, *c.1942. Pencil and gouache on paper, 23.5 x 33 cm*

Hepworth, Gabo and Margaret Mellis were all producing across the water, in St Ives, at this time.

The low-lying archipelago where Wells was more or less marooned during the war (he got back to the mainland as soon as he could), with its temperate microclimate and sense of detachment from the rest of Britain, presents a very different visual environment to the cliffs, moors and harbour villages of Cornwall. Visiting the island of Tresco in 1945, the former Surrealist Julian Trevelyan painted the landscape as a storybook place in which the only sign of the great political

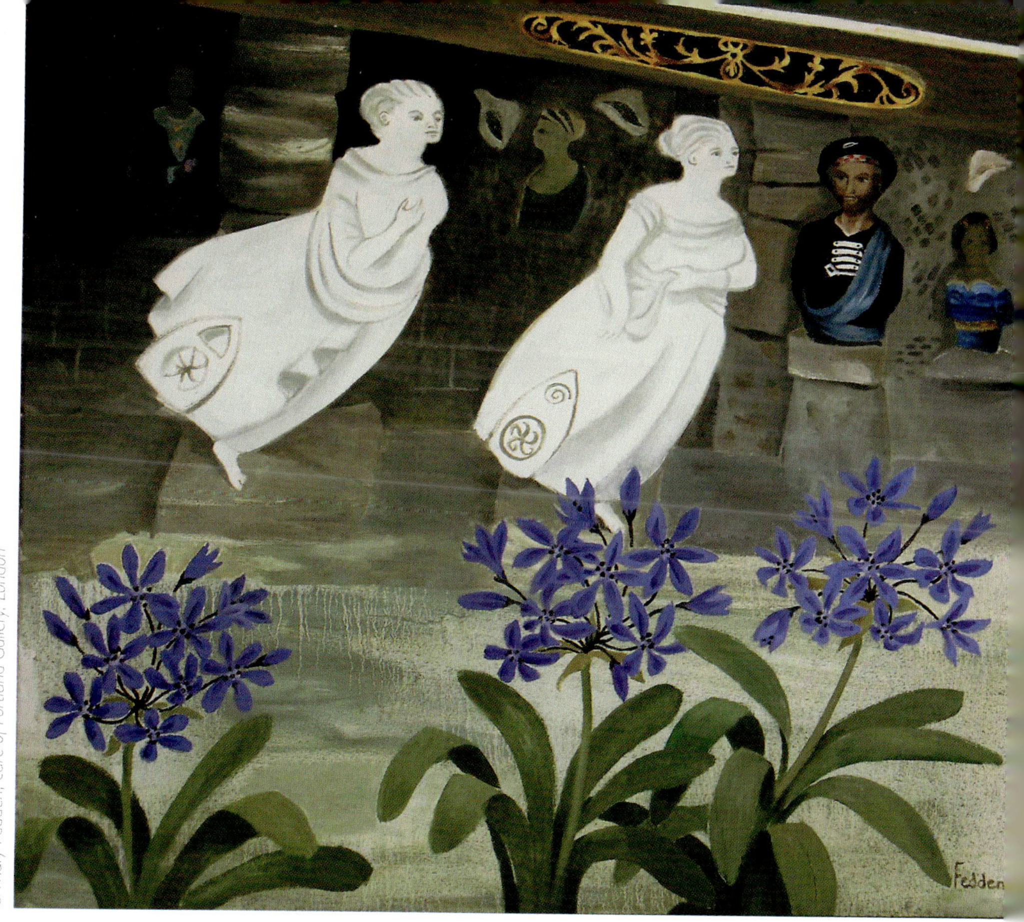

Mary Fedden, 'Valhalla', Abbey Gardens, Tresco, *2003. Oil on canvas, 70 x 80 cm*

events shaping the rest of the world is the Union Jack tugging at its pole on a cottage roof. On a later trip to Tresco in 2003, Mary Fedden (Trevelyan's wife) painted 'Valhalla', a little open-air museum of figureheads salvaged from shipwrecks on the Isles of Scilly. These beautifully carved ghosts of tragic events seem to float amid abundant agapanthus flowers in the Abbey Garden. It was probably around 1953 that Winifred Nicholson too had stayed as a guest in Tresco Abbey, where she painted the view from a bedroom in the tower (left). Beyond the gate (a feature that often appears, like a symbol, in her work), a track stretches straight to the dunes, as though reaching seawards, pointing towards the Eastern Isles and the return voyage to mainland Cornwall.

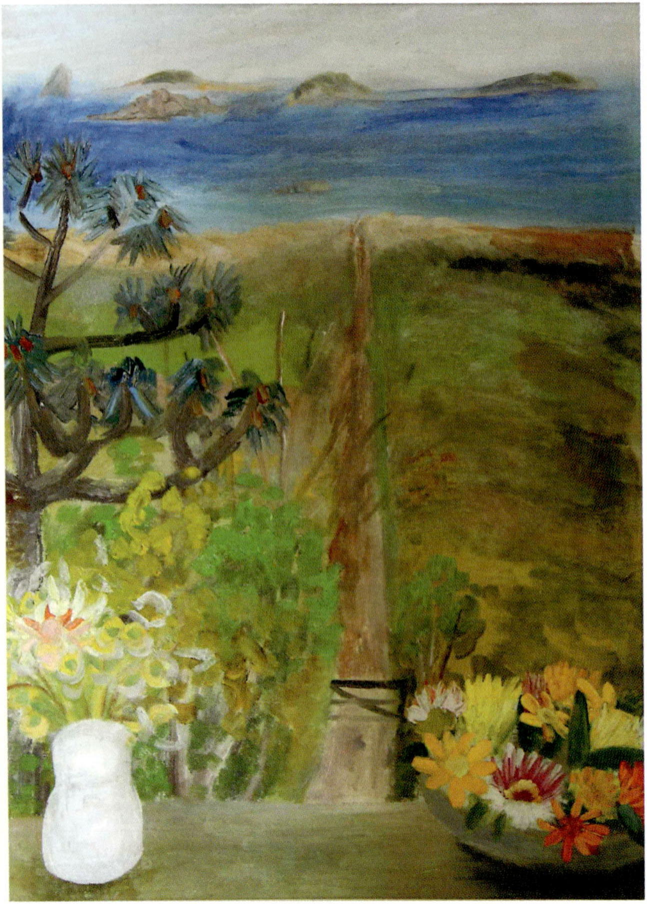

Winifred Nicholson, View from a Window: Path to the Coast, c.*1953.*
Oil on canvas board, 57 x 41.5 cm

St Just to St Ives, across the Penwith Moors

Setting out from Land's End along the north coast of the Penwith peninsula, the first town you hit is St Just. From ancient times this was one of the most productive centres of Cornish tin and copper mining: at nearby Botallack, Levant, Trewellard and Pendeen deep mineworks extend far out under the seabed. Roofless engine houses and decaying chimneys cluster on the cliffs like abandoned citadels, while spoil heaps roughly skinned with vegetation lie everywhere underfoot. In St Just itself, the artist David Haughton was captivated by the regular yet asymmetrical perspectives created by the tight-knit terraces of miners' cottages. 'The turning point in my life,' he declared, 'occurred when I first discovered the town of St Just'. Haughton trained at the Slade School in the 1940s with Feiler and Wynter; on moving to Cornwall in 1947, he went further west than most of his contemporaries, who tended to settle around St Ives. Even after returning to London in 1951, he made yearly visits to paint in St Just.

From 1960 until his death in 2005 Karl Weschke lived at nearby Cape Cornwall. 'I came here because it was very cheap,' he insisted. 'People are always surprised that I don't say it was because of the light.' Weschke had little interest in the kind of abstract art associated with Hepworth and Nicholson. Before he first came to Cornwall in 1955, Weschke had travelled in Spain, where he met members of the London-based Borough Group, whose mentor was David Bomberg (page 93). In Weschke's large paintings the dark rhythms of this landscape often cradle a human drama of threat or isolation. *Body on the Beach* alludes to a diving accident in which Weschke was forced to make a rapid and perilous ascent from deep water. In *Cape Cornwall* (1960; page 80) the land's contours swell and fold as though under pressure from the human histories enacted beneath them.

The hauntingly monumental dereliction of this post-industrial landscape provided the setting for anarchic open-air productions by Kneehigh Theatre Company in the

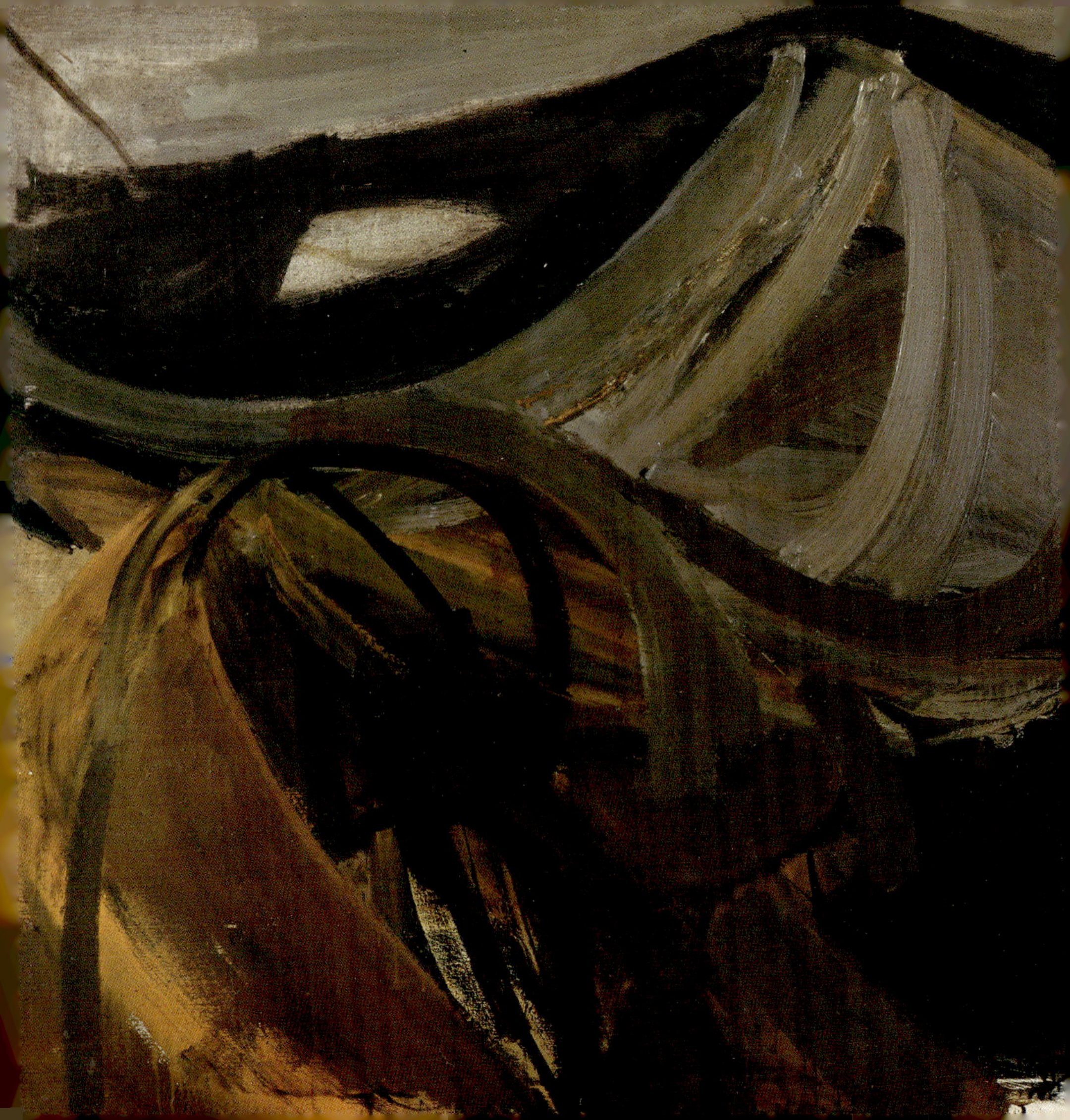

1990s, for which the artist David Kemp created colossal props out of junk. Kemp assembles found objects of all kinds – boots, computer boards, brushes, engines, wheels – into sculptures that look as though they have been discovered by archaeologists at ancient ritual sites (page 83). In a sense they have, since Kemp refers to these works as 'Relics, Artefacts and God Dollies from the Consumer Cults that thrived on the South West Peninsula at the end of the Second Millennium'. 'Living among the ruins,' he says, 'I collect the fragments, piecing together some curious connections between the past and emergent mythologies and technologies.'

There's a different connection between ancient and modern artefacts in the sculptures of Paul Mount, another long-time resident of the St Just area, who settled there in 1962 after seven years in Lagos. In Nigeria Mount's architectural designs and wood sculptures had been shaped by both European modernism and the rich West African sculptural traditions. In Cornwall, he translated his ideas into metal, learning to weld from a local blacksmith, and scavenging steel offcuts from metalworks in Hayle. Like William Scott, he was more excited by man-made forms than natural ones. He drew the mechanical gear on fishing boats in Newlyn harbour, which he said 'introduced a great many forms into my work that I wouldn't have thought of otherwise'. Mount's stainless steel works look almost mathematical, with their geometric shapes, yet their reflective surfaces also allow the environment to become part of the sculpture (page 82).

Of all the artists who have worked in this area, its most notorious resident – though he didn't paint its buildings, landscape or people – was Roger Hilton. During the 1950s Hilton made extended working visits from London to Cornwall. Like Frost, Heron, Lanyon and Wynter, with whom his work regularly appeared in exhibitions at that time, he was experimenting with gestural abstract painting – an art form he described in epic terms. 'The abstract painter,' he wrote, 'submits himself entirely to the unknown… he is like a man swinging out into the void.' In 1965 Hilton moved with his new wife, Rose, and young family to a cottage on the edge of the mining settlement of Botallack.

Unpredictable, outrageous, fiercely intelligent and incorrigibly provocative, Hilton left a vast local legacy of risqué anecdotes as well as hundreds of paintings in gouache on paper that

Facing page: Karl Weschke, Cape Cornwall, *1960. Oil on canvas, 122 x 122 cm*

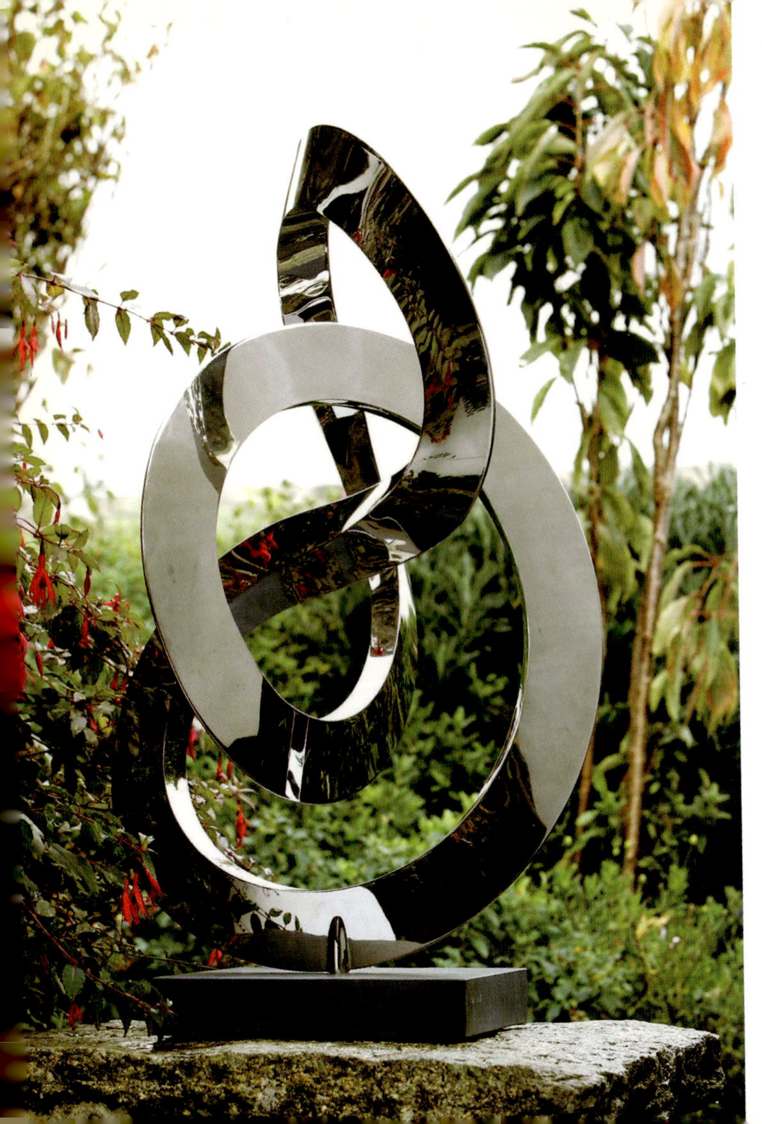

Paul Mount, Ewigkeit, *2008. Stainless steel, 86 x 50 cm*

Courtesy of Beaux Arts and the Paul Mount Estate

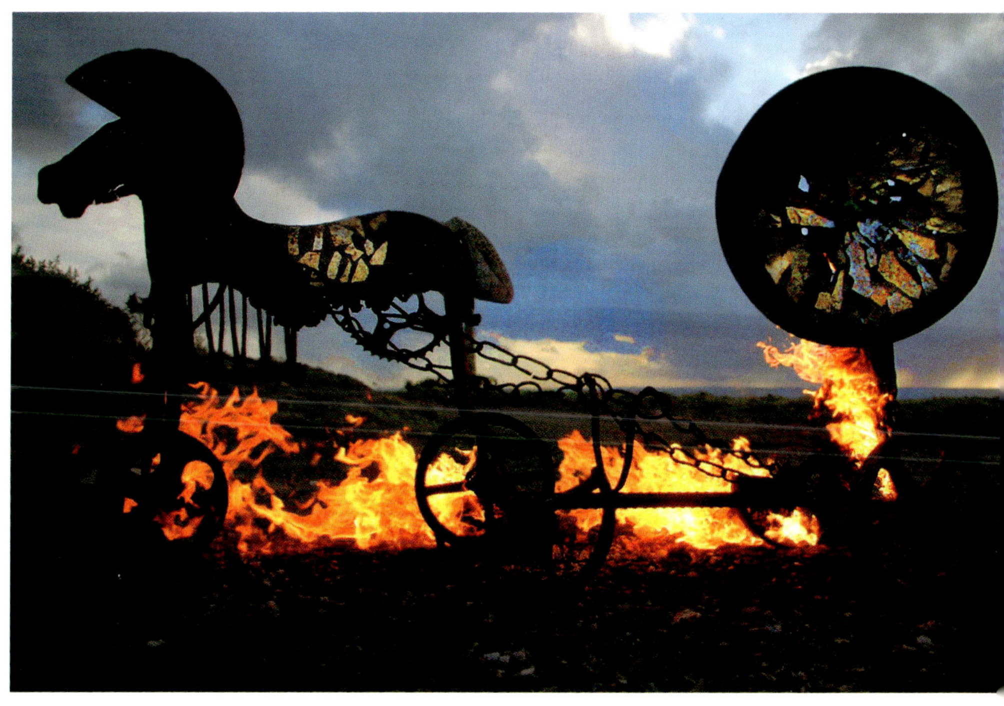

David Kemp, Fire Chariot, *1997, at Botallack. Assemblage of found objects, 80 x 140 x 40 cm*

he produced during the early 1970s, when he was almost unable to leave his bed as a result of neuritis brought on by alcoholism. These gouaches are populated by fantasy animals and erotic scenes, and sometimes by boats that seem to symbolize the possibility of voyaging to other worlds, beyond the sea horizon just visible from the cottage windows (page 84). A couple of years before Hilton's death in 1975, Rose tentatively began to resume her own artistic career. It was a painting of Roger on his sickbed, in which the walls are a pulsing red reminiscent of Matisse, that Rose considered 'my first satisfactory painting

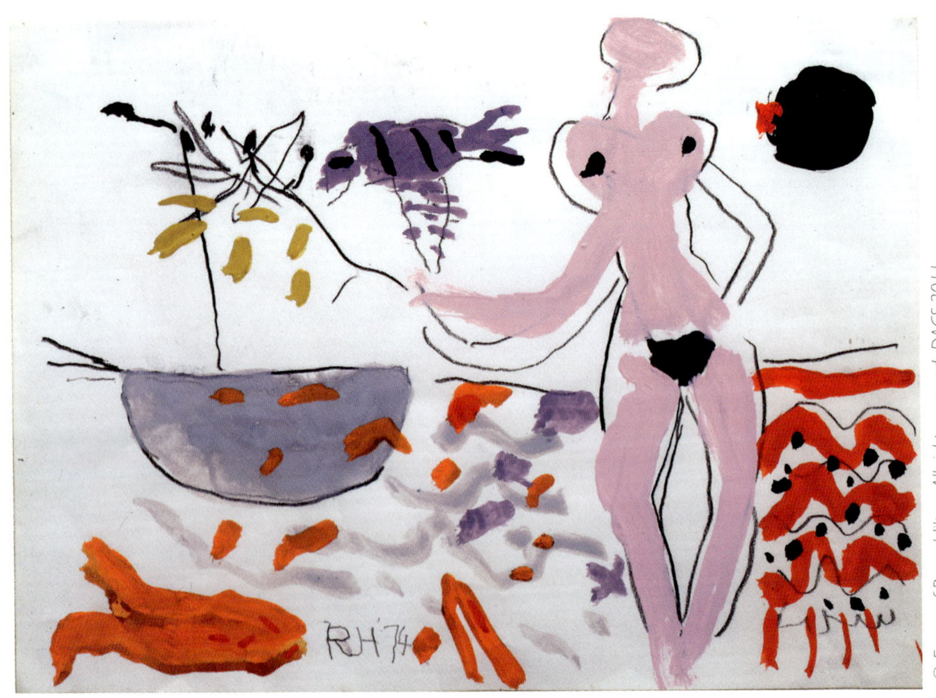

Roger Hilton, Pink Nude with Bird, Boat and Black Sun, *1974. Gouache and charcoal on paper, 30.5 x 47.5 cm*

of colour being used positively'. In her *Botallack Landscape* (2008; page 85) the bare, lumpy contours that register in Weschke's *Cape Cornwall* are there, but transformed by a gentle intensity of colour into a place that feels much warmer and more benign – a habitation rather than a habitat.

The narrow coast road eastwards from Botallack dips and winds along the edge of the Penwith moors. Geologically these granite uplands form a small, compact extension

Facing page: Rose Hilton, Botallack Landscape, *2008. Oil on canvas, 76.2 x 76.2 cm*

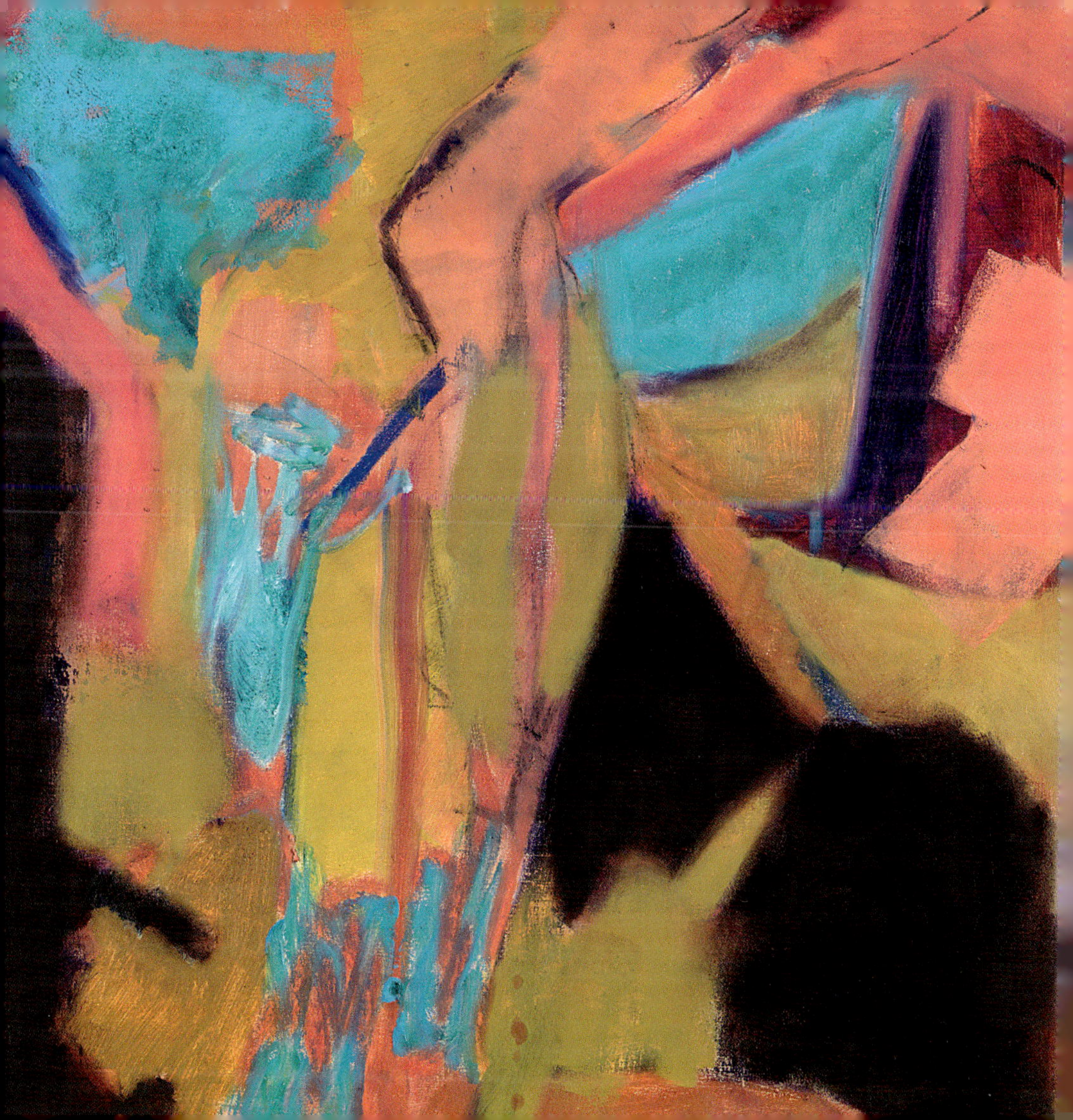

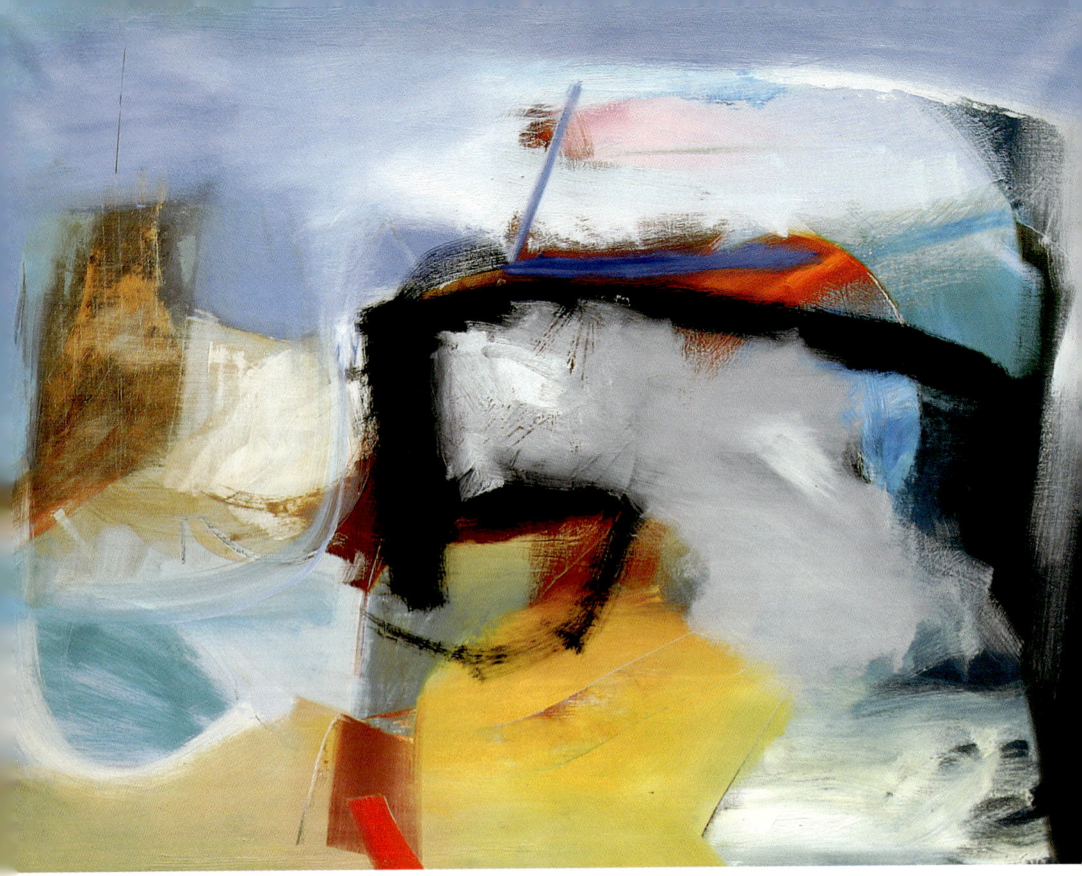

Matthew Lanyon, Bosigran V, *2005. Oil on canvas, 122 x 91.5 cm*

of Dartmoor and Bodmin Moor. From their high points the sea is visible, not far away, on both sides. And, though there are places where moors (the local word is downs) seem wild and empty, the signs of past industry and settlement are everywhere. The prehistoric drystone walls that encircle many fields are thought to be the oldest man-made structures in the world still being used for their original purpose. There are ancient hut circles and standing stones, mineworkings and clay pits, overgrown trackways and derelict farmsteads. Much of the work that is usually labelled 'St Ives art' was produced by artists who lived and worked out here, some distance from the town. Whereas Cornwall's Victorian art colonists liked their clubs and societies, the feeling of belonging to a group with shared aims, the pattern in the twentieth century was different. The artist became instead a lone explorer, an outsider and breaker of rules. The little harbour town of St Ives didn't altogether fit with this kind of artistic persona. Somewhere wilder, rougher, more on the fringes was needed. When people talk about the influence of the Cornish landscape on artists, it's often this landscape that they mean.

Along the coast road you keep passing farmsteads and villages whose names have found their way into art. *Bojewyan Farms* is the title of one of Peter Lanyon's 1952 'St Just' series of paintings, a place that he enthusiastically noted 'stinks of dung', the stuff of real experience rather than abstract art theory. Futher on, the cliff at Bosigran – famed among rock climbers – recurs in the titles of works by Peter's son Matthew Lanyon: 'It's a great beast of a place, full of surprise, totally vertigo, scary and exciting'. This feeling comes through in Lanyon's 'Bosigran' image of a jutting, angular form like an overhang from which red brushmarks seem to tumble in a movement of exhilaration and danger (page 86). Further still, you reach Gurnard's Head, where the poet and friend of artists W.S. Graham lived precariously in a coastguard's cottage from 1956 to 1962. Then Zennor – a church, a pub and a few houses in a dip of the moors, circled by outlying farms – which has been home since the 1900s to a remarkable number of artists and writers.

D.H. Lawrence described the view from the cliffs at Zennor across the 'infinite Atlantic, all peacock-mingled colour' as 'lovelier even than the Mediterranean'. When he arrived in 1915, Lawrence was searching for his own version of a life in tune with natural desires and not distorted by convention. He was briefly convinced that he had found it at Zennor, where he fantasized about communing with ancestral Celtic spirits on the Penwith moors. This theme is a familiar refrain in later artists' and writers' responses to the landscape. For some, such as Sven Berlin, it became their creative credo; others took it less seriously. The poet John Heath-Stubbs, who in the late 1940s trod a well-worn trail

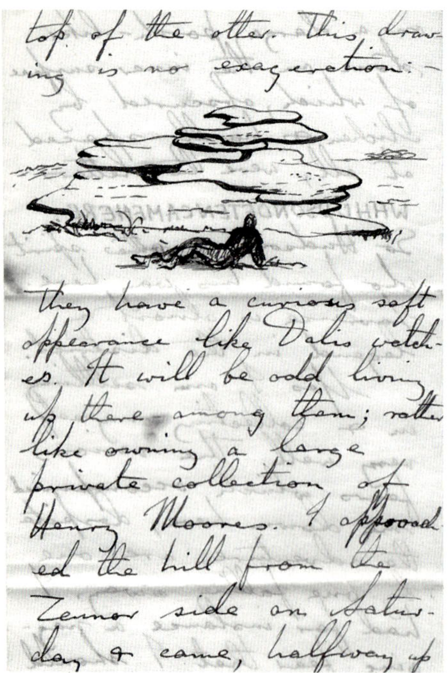
top of the other. This draw-
ing is no exageration:-

they have a curious soft
appearance like Dalis watches. It will be odd living
up there among them; rather
like owning a large
private collection of
Henry Moores. I approach-
ed the hill from the
Zennor side on Satur-
day & came, halfway up

Bryan Wynter, a page from a letter to Hedy Hoffmann, 1945

between literary London and west Cornwall, jokingly christened Zennor 'the sea coast of Bohemia'. His poem about the medieval carving of a mermaid in the parish church describes her native land as 'a hideous and wicked country', shadowed by memories of pagan rituals and human sacrifice.

Eager to make a new start after the war, Bryan Wynter found a decaying cottage known as the Carn in the lee of a bare outcrop above Zennor, where he lived from 1945 to 1964. The exposed rock piles, eroded over millennia by frost and rain, reminded him of the Surrealist art he admired. 'They have a curious soft appearance like Dali's watches', he wrote. 'It will be odd living up there among them' (left). Sometimes it seemed to him impossible to distinguish the actual landscape from the strong feelings it aroused, the images it suggested: 'The real landscape overflows into the unconscious & the unconscious wells up peopling the real landscape with its own images. This is particularly so at dusk when the rocks and gorse shapes seem to come alive.' Wynter practised Surrealist methods of automatism, in which the artist allows chance rather than intention to inform their work. In *Zennor Coast from the Sea* (page 89) he used a technique called decalcomania, which involves pressing two inked or painted surfaces together, pulling them apart and using the resulting, accidental shapes and textures. He'd probably meant to paint a landscape of some kind, but the exact location and the form of the fissured rocks came about through automatism.

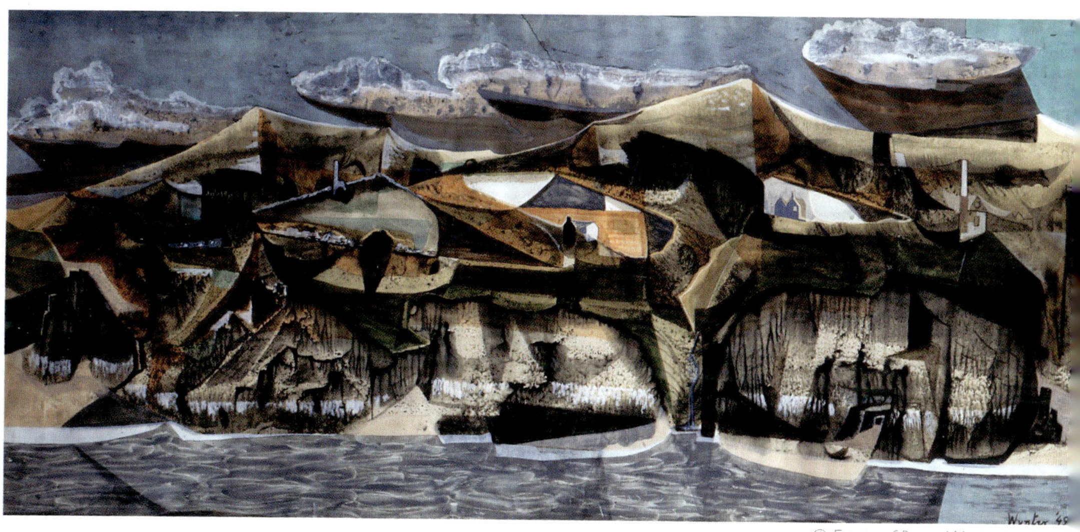

Bryan Wynter, Zennor Coast from the Sea, *1949. Monotype and gouache on paper, 33 x 73.5 cm*

Across the seaward slope of the moors, Wynter's cottage overlooked the imposing gabled bulk of Eagles Nest (page 90), which in early 1956 became the new home of his friend and fellow artist Patrick Heron. Heron's links with St Ives went back to childhood in the late 1920s, when his entrepreneur father Tom Heron managed the textile works above Porthmeor Beach where the fashionable Crysède silks were printed. The family had stayed for several weeks at Eagles Nest, then owned by the Labour politician and artist Will Arnold-Forster. This place enthralled Heron – but, he agonized, would relocating here from London turn out to be a bold creative move or simply an escapist 'return to the womb'?

In the event, Heron found that his new environment had an immediate effect on his art. The very air of Cornwall, he was convinced, 'contains more light than in England: light reflected up and off the sea'. It reminded him of the light of Provence, in the paintings he loved by Matisse and Bonnard. As the azaleas in the sub-tropical garden around the house burst into bloom, he embarked on a series of 'Garden Paintings'. In these works, a modern French style of tachiste painting

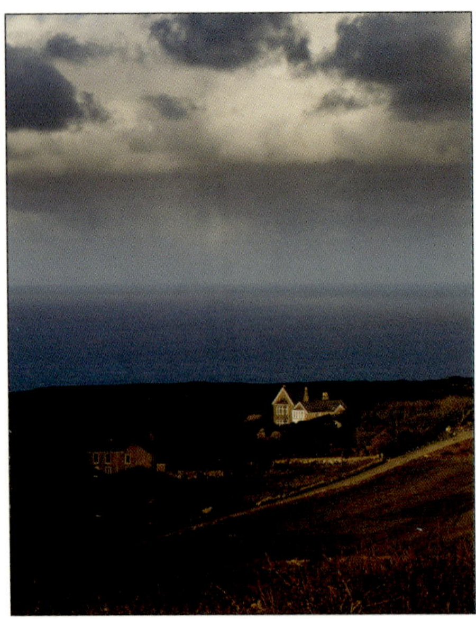

Eagles Nest from Zennor Hill, winter

(emphasizing the freeform marks, or *taches*, made by the artist's brush) fused with the colours and atmosphere of the garden (page 91). Heron and his wife Delia were generous hosts. As had happened when Adrian Stokes and Margaret Mellis moved down to Carbis Bay in 1939, the Herons' guests included a constant stream of visitors from London's cultural élite, which helped to draw renewed attention to artistic activity in west Cornwall.

Below Eagles Nest stands the little row of cottages called Higher Tregerthen, once tenanted by Lawrence and Frieda. When Trevor Bell moved out in 1957, his cottage was taken by Sandra Blow, who had been among the Herons' house guests that Easter and had decided to stay on in this curiously stimulating outpost of the metropolitan art world with which she was familiar. Since her early encounters with Italian and American abstract artists in the 1940s, Blow had developed a form of abstract 'matter painting' that incorporated collage materials such as sacking and plaster. She worked outdoors, propping her boards against a barn wall. She recalled how once 'a flock of sheep stood behind me and watched as I worked. A farmer watching from a distance said he'd never seen anything like it.' In *Cornwall* (1958; page 92), painted swathes of sacking echo the texture and rhythm of the landscape, as though simultaneously seen from a distance and as a close, sensory experience.

Some years earlier David Bomberg had explored this same area on a summer visit in 1947, when he camped by Trendrine Hill between Zennor and St Ives. At the start of his career, before the First World War, Bomberg was associated with the radical Vorticist group, who believed that the new,

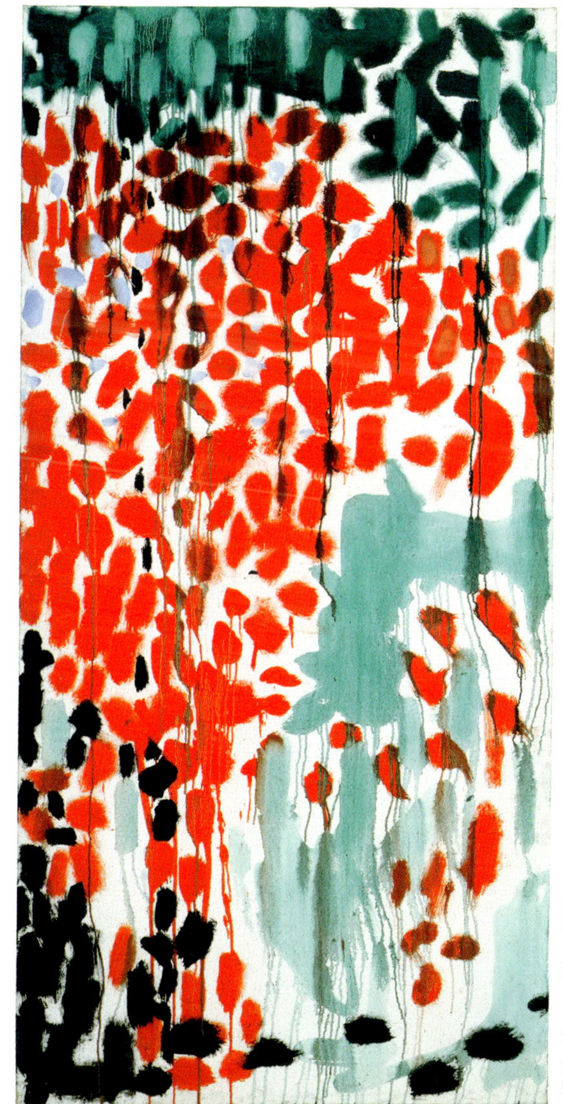

Patrick Heron,
Summer Painting: August 1956,
1956. Oil on canvas, 183 x 91 cm

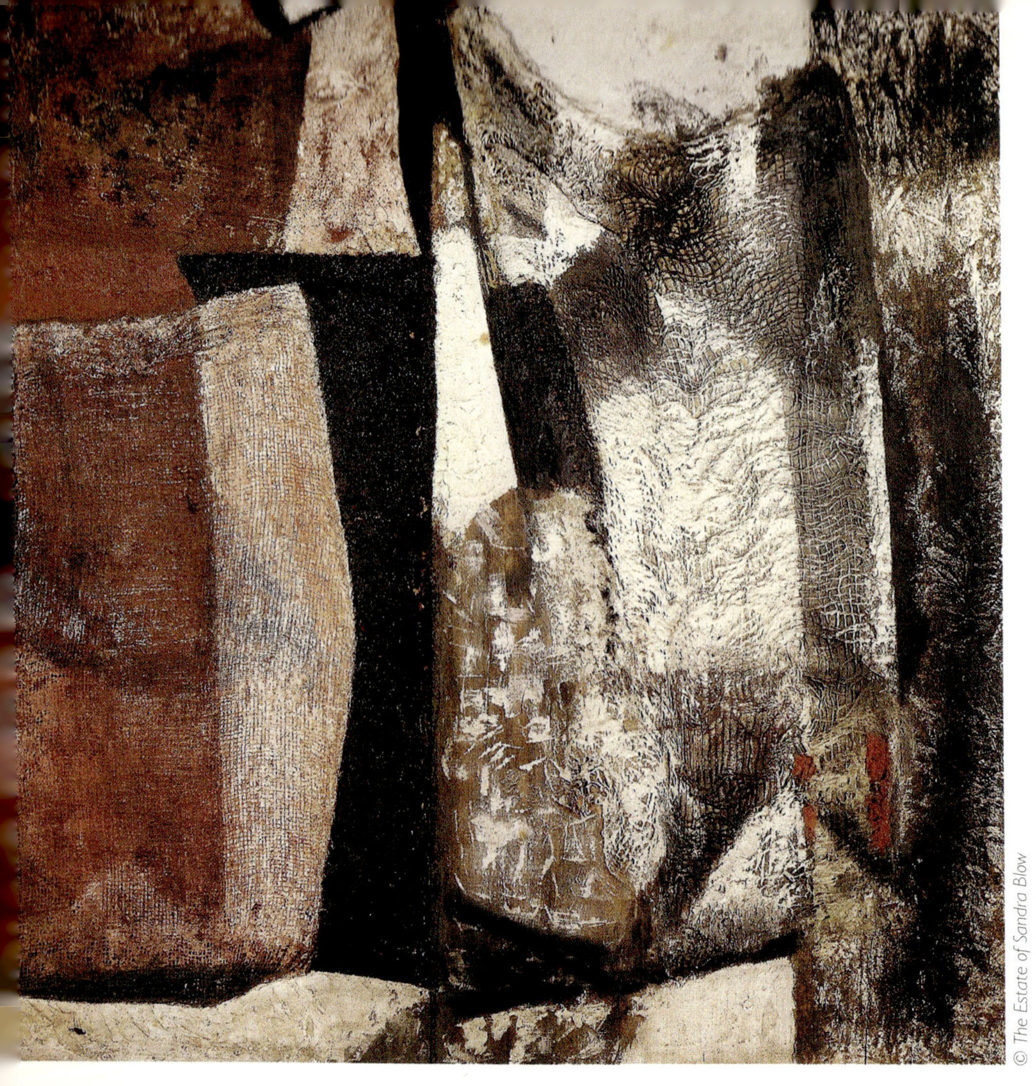

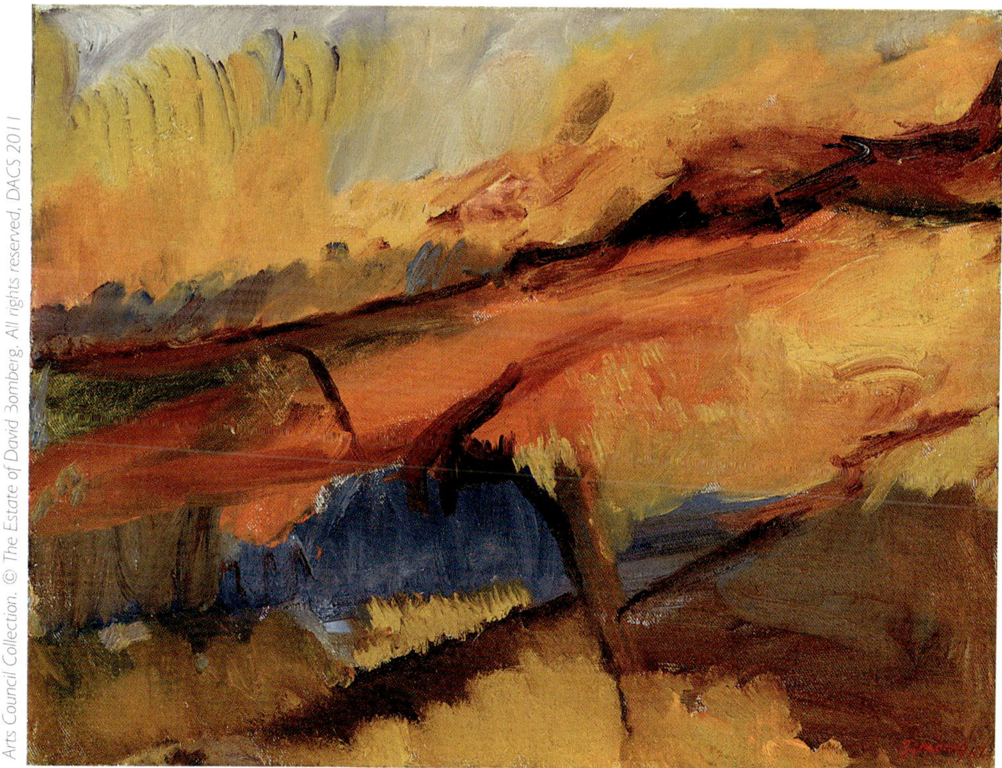

David Bomberg, Trendrine, *1947. Oil on canvas, 81.3 x 106.7 cm*

twentieth-century machine age demanded an angular, dynamic art. He later developed a freer, more expressionistic style, but remained concerned with structure and vitality in painting. What he called 'the spirit in the mass' can be felt in his paintings of Cornwall. Between the wars, Bomberg had worked in Palestine and Spain, and his *Trendrine* has the baked, oxidized tones of Mediterranean

Facing page: Sandra Blow, Cornwall, *1958. Oil, plaster and sacking on board, 119.4 x 110.5 cm*

soil (page 93). Landscape and abstract forms almost merge; this is supposedly a typical feature of 'St Ives art', but Bomberg was never socially or professionally connected to the art world in Cornwall, and for this reason he hardly ever features in its story.

Past Trendrine the road climbs again, to the hill of Trevalgan (title of a 1956 sculpture by Hepworth and a 1951 painting by Peter Lanyon, as well as the site of a memorial to him), before dropping into a long downhill run towards St Ives and the bay beyond. As it leaves the Penwith moors behind, the road enters St Ives along the valley of the Stennack, or 'tin ground'. This is where Bernard Leach and Shoji Hamada set about constructing a three-chambered oriental kiln in 1920, in what were then open fields. Far from supplies of wood, suitable clays or outlets for sales, it was the last place in the world you could imagine making a commercial success of a craft pottery. Yet the successors to Leach's first kiln and the house he built next to it were to become a place of international ceramic pilgrimage. Fragments of misfired or imperfect pots joined debris from the farms and mines on the bed of the Stennack stream where they were thrown.

St Ives and the North Coast

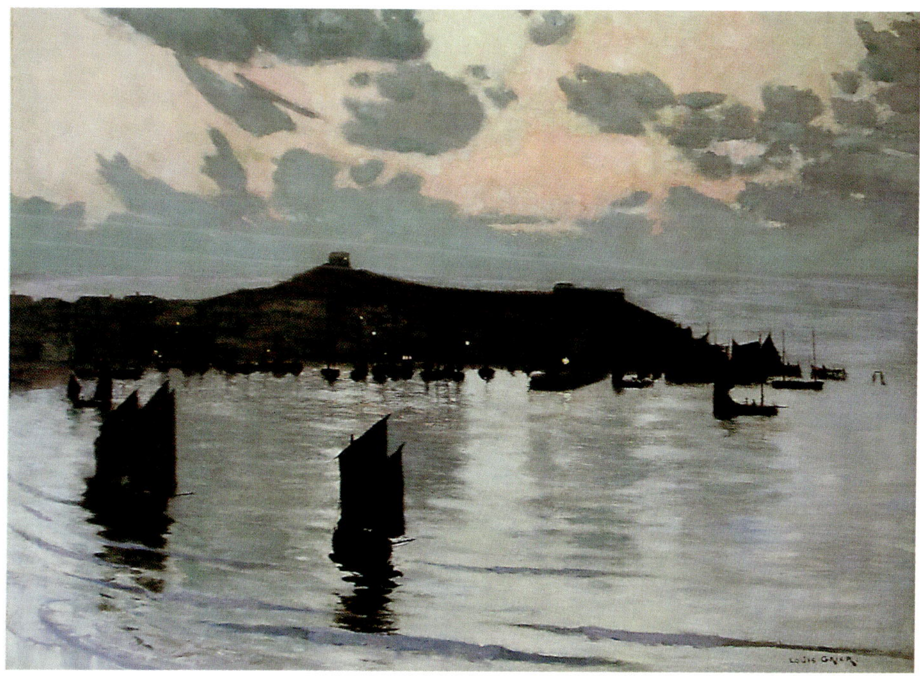

Louis Monro Grier, Twilight, St Ives, *c.1890. Oil on canvas, 75.5 x 101 cm*

Down into St Ives. On the lower slopes of the Stennack, Turner paused on his 1811 West Country tour to make a few quick drawings of the town that at that date hardly extended beyond the harbour. From the hillside he could see across the clustered

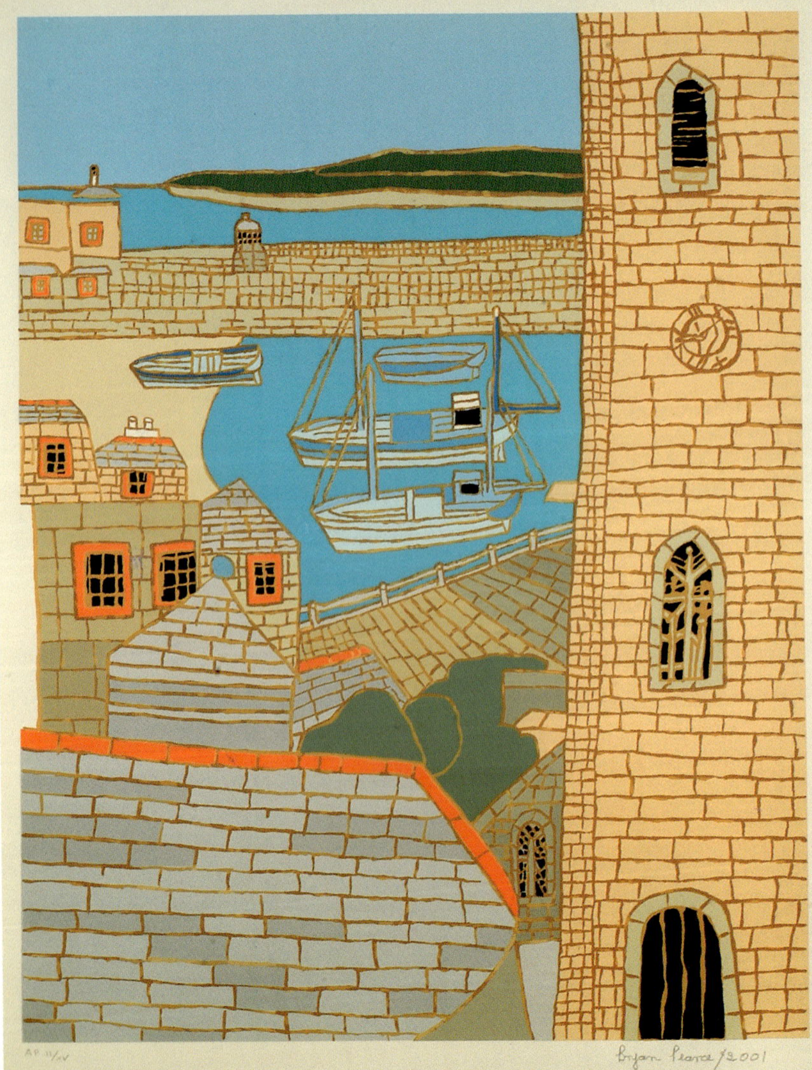
Bryan Pearce /2001

rooftops to the medieval church tower and its four stubby pinnacles, carved from obdurate granite that resisted any attempt at fine detail. In the foreground a watermill creaked and splashed. The view he recorded is still recognizable, though the watermill has gone and St Ives has expanded all the way up to Leach's pottery.

Where the valley reaches the sea, the parish church of St Ia stands on the cusp of the harbour. In the Lady Chapel, Barbara Hepworth's *Madonna and Child* (1953) commemorates the death of her eldest son, Paul, on a military flight over Thailand. The consolation Hepworth sought in her feeling for landscape can be seen even in this figure sculpture, in the wavelike folds in the Virgin's mantle. The church building, with its stones, slates and windowpanes lovingly itemized, features repeatedly in Bryan Pearce's work. Born in St Ives, Pearce sustained brain damage as a result of the rare condition phenylketonuria. His paintings are often praised with the word 'naïve', although they are hardly more naïve than the magnificent medieval murals in the church at Breage. In Pearce's St Ives, every detail slots together, as though providing a complete, satisfying system for looking at and thinking about his home town.

Facing page: Bryan Pearce, St Ives Church from the Market, *2001. Screenprint on paper, 56 x 44.5 cm*

The far side of the harbour is bounded by Smeaton's Pier – named for the eighteenth-century civil engineer John Smeaton – with its distinctive squat, domed lighthouse. Throughout the following century this little arena was packed with the russet sails of pilchard boats, a sight the gentlemen artists were just in time to catch in the 1880s before the fishing industry slipped into decline. Their enthusiasm sounds faintly predatory in a local historian's account of summer 1885, when artists from far afield 'swooped down on St Ives with the intention of making it their abode and field of labour'. Among them was the Australian painter Louis Monro Grier, who observed the comings and goings of the fleet from his harbourside studio. In his *Twilight, St Ives* (c.1890; page 95), the lights along the wharf pulse brighter each moment as darkness falls. This was the kind of lyrical, atmospheric effect associated with Whistler, who had passed through St Ives some six years earlier and whom Grier admired. Close to Grier's studio is the building that in 1890 became St Ives Artists' Club, a gathering place and watering hole for the town's new colonists, where they could recreate the civilized social routines they'd enjoyed in their city lives.

Sixty years later the shapes and colours of the St Ives quayside were reflected quite differently in abstract paintings by Terry Frost. Soon after settling in St Ives in 1946, Frost began a termly commute to art school in London, where he'd enlisted under the government scheme for ex-servicemen and trained in realist painting. Back in St Ives, he practised his observational drawing around the harbour, filling notebooks with sketches of boats and people. But it was not until he made his first abstract works that he felt he'd found a visual idiom of his own. The rocking, curved forms in these paintings and the lines connecting them clearly relate to the shapes of boats, masts and ropes in St Ives harbour. Of the painting he regarded as his real breakthrough, *Walk Along the Quay*, he told the following story. To prevent neighbours in the flats near the quayside from being woken by the crying of his youngest child, Frost pushed the baby in its pram along Smeaton's Pier. The feeling of this movement, together with the sight of the boats moored by the wall, found expression in a long, narrow painting. When Frost rotated the picture upright, any references to curved hulls, a horizon line or the route of a walk were transformed into a purely abstract composition. The 'Walk Along the Quay' theme and the half-moon motif (boat, pram or pure geometry) occur many times in Frost paintings in the early 1950s and throughout his later career (page 99).

Either side of the harbour, St Ives's two long, sandy beaches, Porthminster to the east and Porthmeor to the west, aroused slightly unequal levels of artistic fervour. Lying directly below the railway station and the early, grand hotels, Porthminster was thoroughly colonized by tourists before the artists could stake their claim. In August 1928, in the afterglow of his first day-trip with Kit Wood, Ben Nicholson brought Winifred and their son, Jake, over to St Ives for a more extended visit; soon after their arrival, he made drawings on both beaches. In his sketch of Porthminster, the town seems to crowd in on the sands, where a pony or donkey is being ridden into an ebbing sea. On Porthmeor he drew Winifred, her back towards him, gazing out towards the wide, unobstructed Atlantic horizon beside their two empty deckchairs. The surf for which Porthmeor is now prized can be seen curling along the shoreline. On the beach's landward side, the road leading

Facing: Terry Frost, Walking along the Quay (Blue Movement), *1952. Oil on canvas, 35.5 x 35.5 cm*

Courtesy of Beaux Arts and The Terry Frost Estate

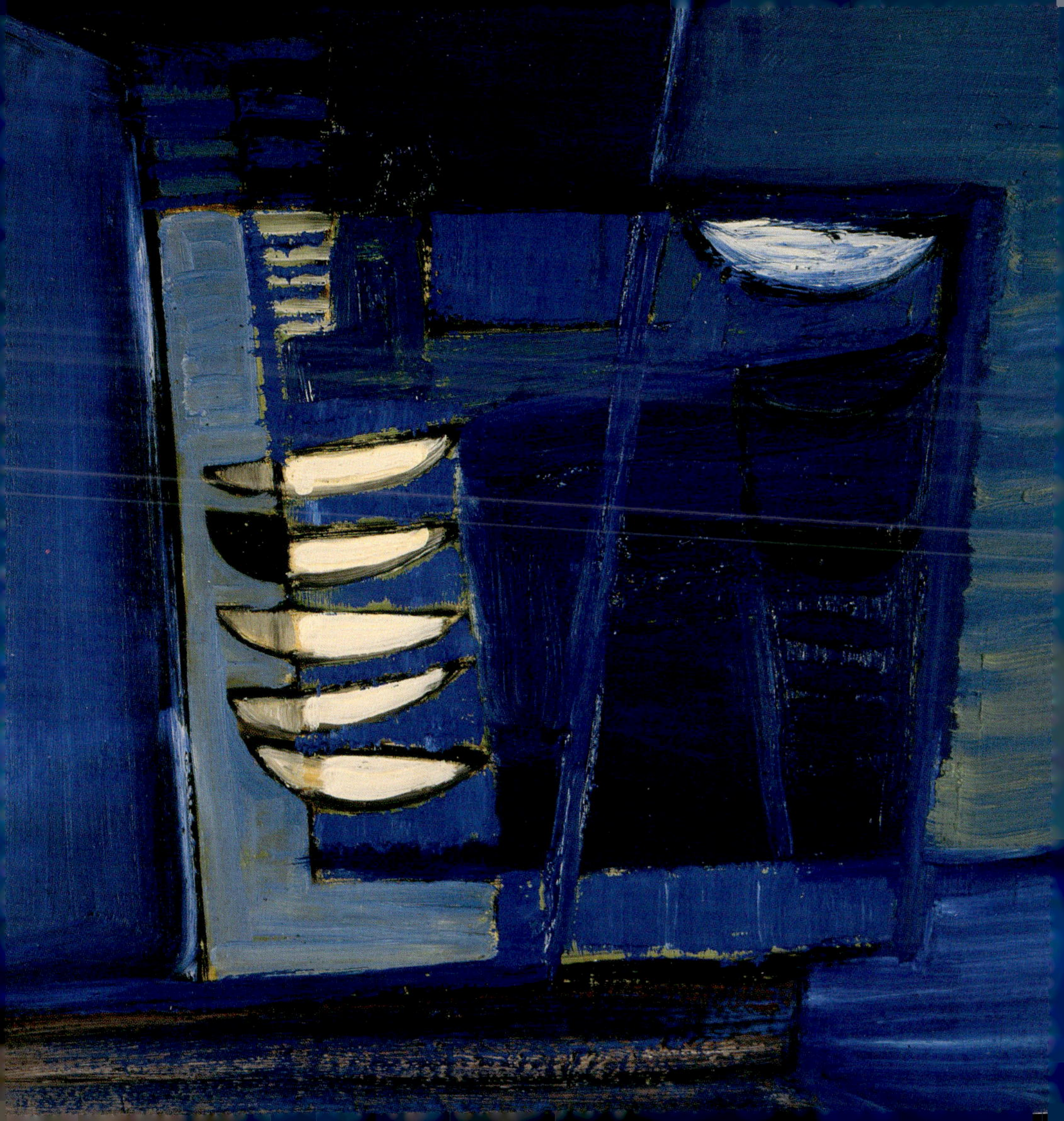

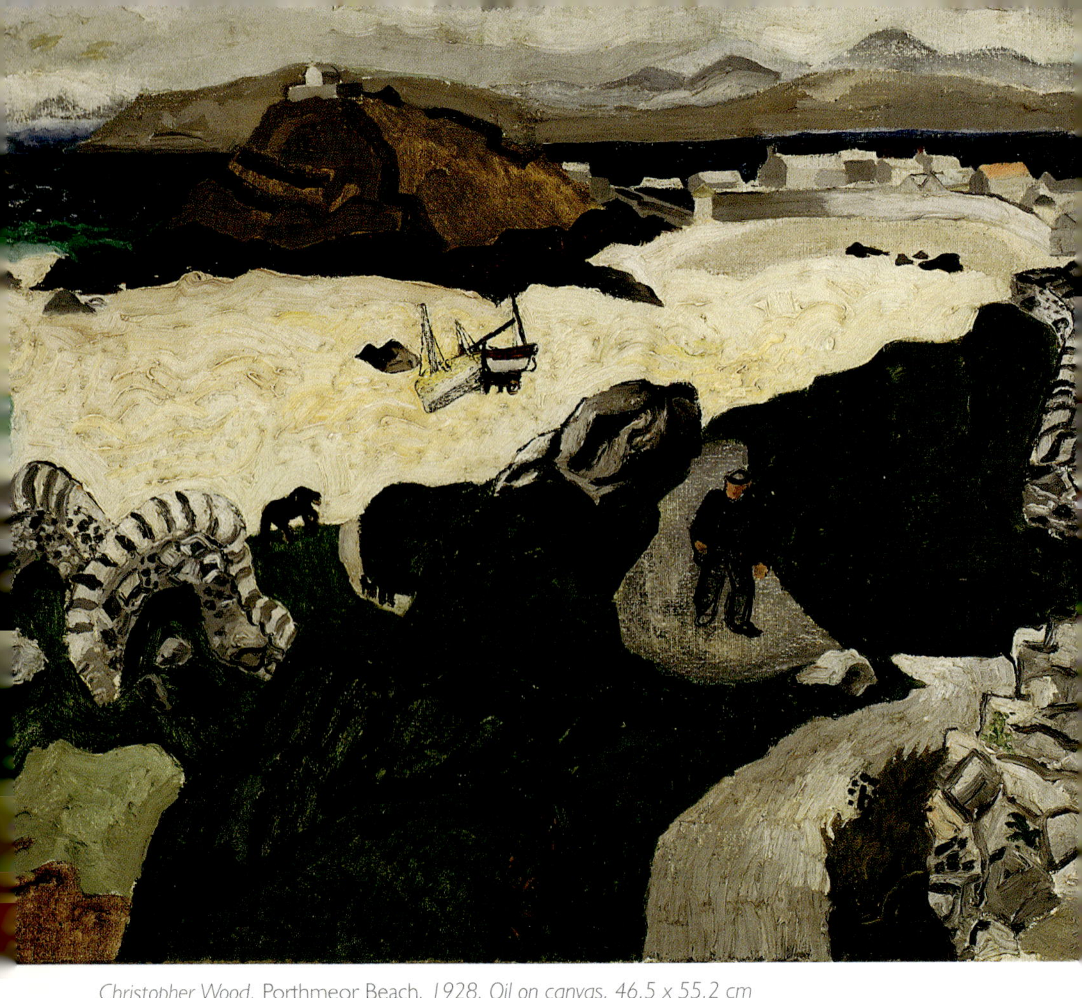

Christopher Wood, Porthmeor Beach, *1928. Oil on canvas, 46.5 x 55.2 cm*

to Wallis's cottage around the corner in Back Road West and the town gasworks (where Tate St Ives now stands) are out of view. Away from the big hotels, this was traditionally the locals' beach, where women spread out their washing on the sand to dry and relatively few tourists ventured.

Kit Wood's painting *Porthmeor Beach* (1928; page 100) reads like a homage to Wallis, painted shortly after their first meeting. Apart from the improbably low tide, it's an accurate topographical view of Porthmeor from the promontory called Man's Head that closes the beach on its western edge. On Porthmeor's far side, the headland known as the Island is crowned by a tiny chapel. Further still, Godrevy lighthouse rises amid the blue of St Ives Bay. In the foreground a hunched figure stomping along the coast path towards us may be Wallis himself, whose favourite recreational walk this was. The urbane Wood, habitué of Parisian salons and friend of Jean Cocteau, had completely fallen for St Ives: 'Each day there is a new thrill here,' he told Winifred Nicholson, 'wonderful sunshine, terrific storms… this place is a picture gallery of only the good pictures.' It sounds too good to be true, although you also catch in his excitement the manic mood swings to which his opium addiction was contributing.

The sculptural texture of the beach, which alters constantly with the tides, fascinated Hepworth. The elongated, muscular form of her bronze *Porthmeor* (1958) echoes the fluid mass and movement of breaking waves. Wilhelmina Barns-Graham's print *Eight Waves on Porthmeor Beach* (1986) consists of eight wavelike horizontal lines that balance and intertwine as though they were a design formed by nature, an elegant graphic restatement of Wood's idea that the landscape here is its own 'picture gallery'. The very name Porthmeor, meaning 'large cove' in Cornish, seemed to cast a spell on artists – it occurs in the titles of innumerable modern paintings and sculptures – but it became St Ives's premier art beach for other reasons too.

Behind the sea wall is a rambling complex of redundant fisheries buildings that by the 1890s was already being given a new lease of life as artists' studios. In a photograph from around this time, Julius Olsson is seated in a camp chair by the window of one of these vast lofts, apparently sketching the view across Porthmeor (page 102). A hammock slung from the rafters and a wicker armchair complete the impression of colonial ease. On verandas throughout the British Empire, men were photographed in similar poses, as though the enjoyment of life's finer pleasures and the

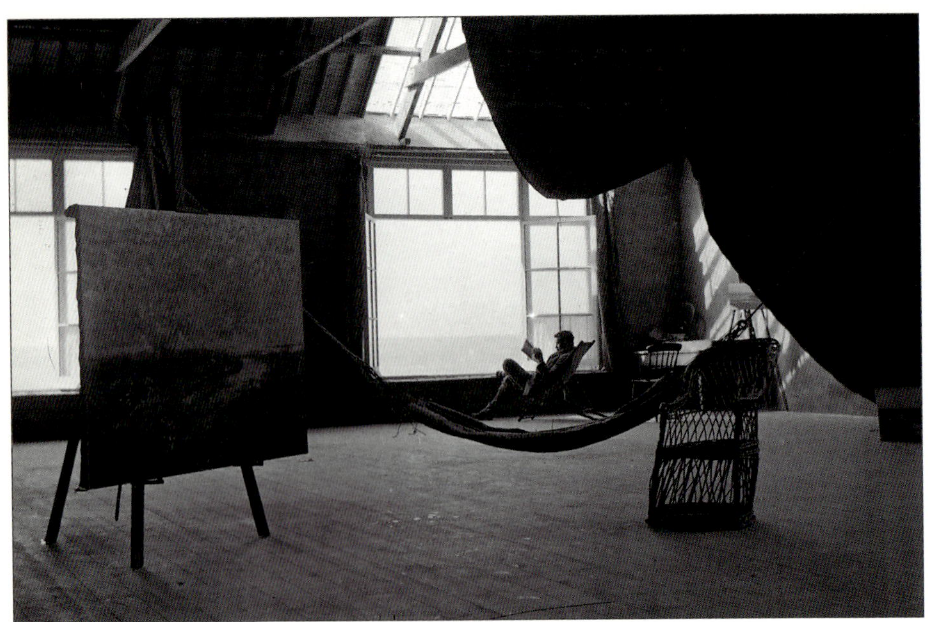

Julius Olsson, seated by a window in Porthmeor Studios, 1890s

right to govern made a seamless whole. A dedicated yachtsman, Olsson was the king of sea painting in St Ives; the many students who passed through his art school there helped to inject a spirit of Porthmeor into the mainstream of British marine painting. The icily sensual effect of his paintings of moonlight on waves combined portentous Victorian grandeur with impressionistic delicacy.

In 1948 the thirteen Porthmeor Studios were bought by a trust set up in memory of Borlase Smart, who had tried hard to open up the St Ives scene to younger, more progressive artists. (In 2012, after years of decay, the building is in the process of being restored.) Studio space in the 1940s was already under pressure from tourist development, and the property boom of the 1990s almost finished off St Ives as a viable place for artists to work. So Porthmeor Studios are (as, in a different sense, they appear in the photo of Olsson) a kind of last frontier. Their tenants can't help but be aware of what goes on outside. Storm tides smash against the windows, summer crowds enjoy the beach oblivious to the art in progress at their backs. These studios have been occupied by many of the artists most closely associated with St Ives, among them Nicholson, Frost, Heron, Tony O'Malley and Trevor Bell – and others, such as Francis Bacon, on whom the name St Ives refuses to stick.

Sandra Blow worked here in the mid-1990s, after being forced out of her Chelsea studio by soaring rents. Thanks to her highly productive year at Tregerthen in 1957–8, Cornwall had positive associations. This time, however, it was the action of the sea rather than the moorland that found its way into her work. Blow's 'Porthmeor' paintings derive their rhythms and colouring from the intricate ridge patterns formed by water flowing through and over the sands: 'When the tide goes out, they're visible, and running across them are inlets of water, which make a sort of grid' (page 104). Ralph Freeman also moved into Porthmeor Studios in the 1990s; in his work too there are abstract structures and patterns that derive from other sources (sometimes the forms of books, documents or architecture), but the colour resonates with what lies beyond the studio windows, as in the atmospheric violet-greys of *Atlantic Verses* (page 105).

It sometimes seems as though the further an artist gets from observational representation, the more pervasive the influence of their surroundings becomes. Trewyn Studio, the workplace-home that Barbara Hepworth bought in 1949 in the centre of St Ives (now open to the public), became much more to her than a space to live and work in (page 106). Discovering the place was, she recalled, 'a kind of magic. For ten years I had passed by with my shopping bags not knowing what lay behind the twenty-foot walls... Here was a studio, a yard and garden where I could work in open air and space.' For the Festival of Britain in 1951, Hepworth was commissioned to produce *Contrapuntal Forms*, a monumental sculpture consisting of two semi-abstract figures. Photographs show her working in the studio garden on a scaffold that resembles an open-air stage. During the following decade, the garden effectively became an environmental theatre for Hepworth's creative philosophy. Together with her friend the

Sandra Blow, Untitled (Porthmeor Series), *1995. Acrylic on canvas, dimensions unknown*

South African composer Priaulx Rainier, then living in St Ives, Hepworth landscaped her domain, planting trees and shrubs among which her sculptures were installed, until this gathering of forms became a kind of alternative family.

From 1945 until her death in a studio fire 30 years later, Hepworth was Britain's most famous female artist (a fact that male artists in St Ives often found hard to stomach). In popular perception, 'St Ives art' came to be identified with her signature style – self-

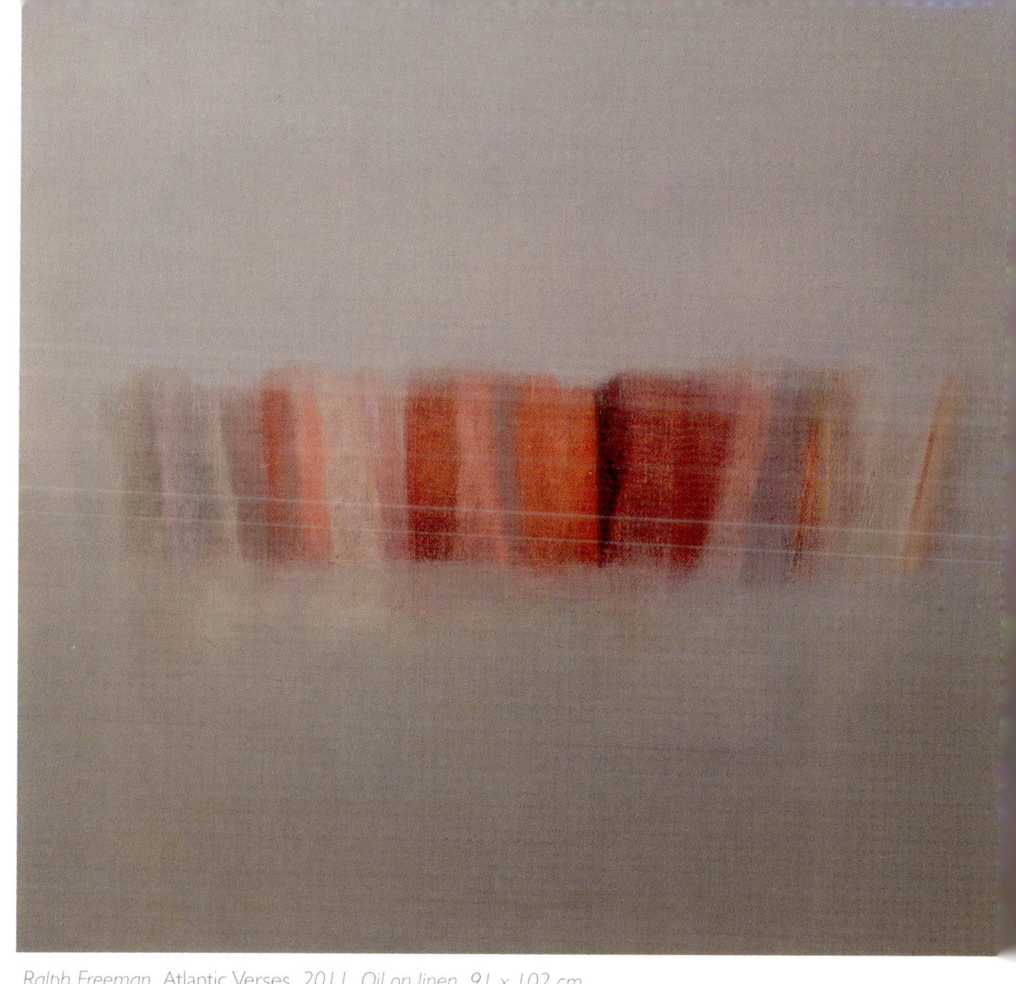

Ralph Freeman, Atlantic Verses, *2011. Oil on linen, 91 x 102 cm*

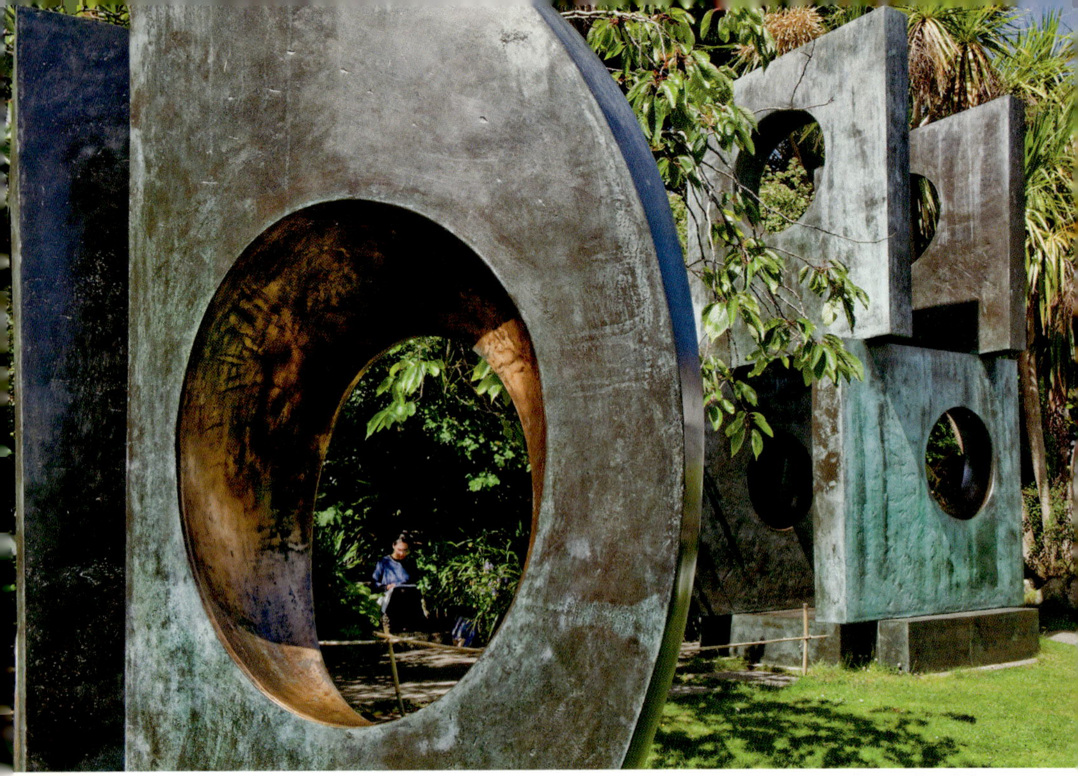

In the garden of Barbara Hepworth's Trewyn Studio, St Ives: (left) Two Forms (Divided Circle), *1969; (right)* Four Square (Walk Through), *1966*

Courtesy Tate St Ives

contained abstract forms, usually pierced by holes and sometimes strung like instruments. This view was underlined for visitors by her numerous sculptures located at strategic points around St Ives: *Epidauros II* near the bus station, overlooking the bay, *Dual Form* outside the Guildhall, *Rock Form (Penwith)* in the public library and *Madonna and Child* in the parish church. Hepworth enabled a succession of younger artists in post-war St Ives to make ends meet by providing employment in her studio, where she increasingly delegated the heavier carving to assistants. As a result of working as Hepworth's chief assistant from 1949 to 1959, Denis Mitchell began to make sculpture himself, first by carving wood and later by casting bronze in sand moulds. Mitchell's bronze sculptures have an evident debt to Hepworth, but they also have a distinctive, flowing sense of uplift, belying the weight of these heavy objects.

'St Ives' is really the wrong label for the modern artists who came to the area during the Second World War, since they actually spent these years in Carbis Bay, a suburban extension that starts at the outskirts of the harbour town and stretches along the coast to the east. It was here that Nicholson, Hepworth and their young triplets stayed as guests of Adrian Stokes and Margaret Mellis at Little Parc Owles, a large house later bought by Peter Lanyon. During their prolonged visit, Nicholson encouraged Mellis, who also had a young son, to get back to making some art of her own. She produced a series of small geometric collages, which at first sight seem typical of the sort of work Nicholson and Gabo had been pursuing in the 1930s. In fact, they are full of wry allusions to Mellis's domestic round of childcare and visitors, in her new role as Cornish hostess to the intelligentsia. In *Blue, Green, Red & Pink Collage* (above) the

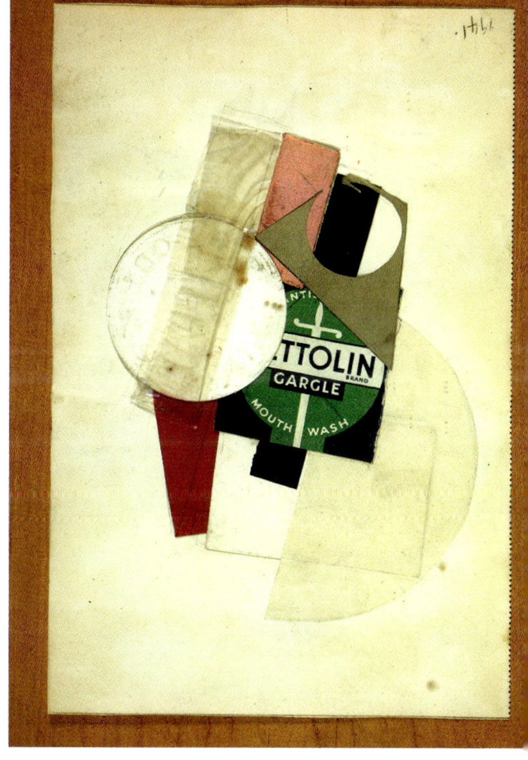

Margaret Mellis, Blue, Green, Red & Pink Collage, *1941. Mixed media on card, 24 x 16 cm*
Photo: Austin Desmond Fine Art, London

'Constructivist' forms are cut from scraps of household rubbish, such as the label from a bottle of Dettolin mouthwash.

Mellis also volunteered to paint camouflage patterns on the tall chimneys of the

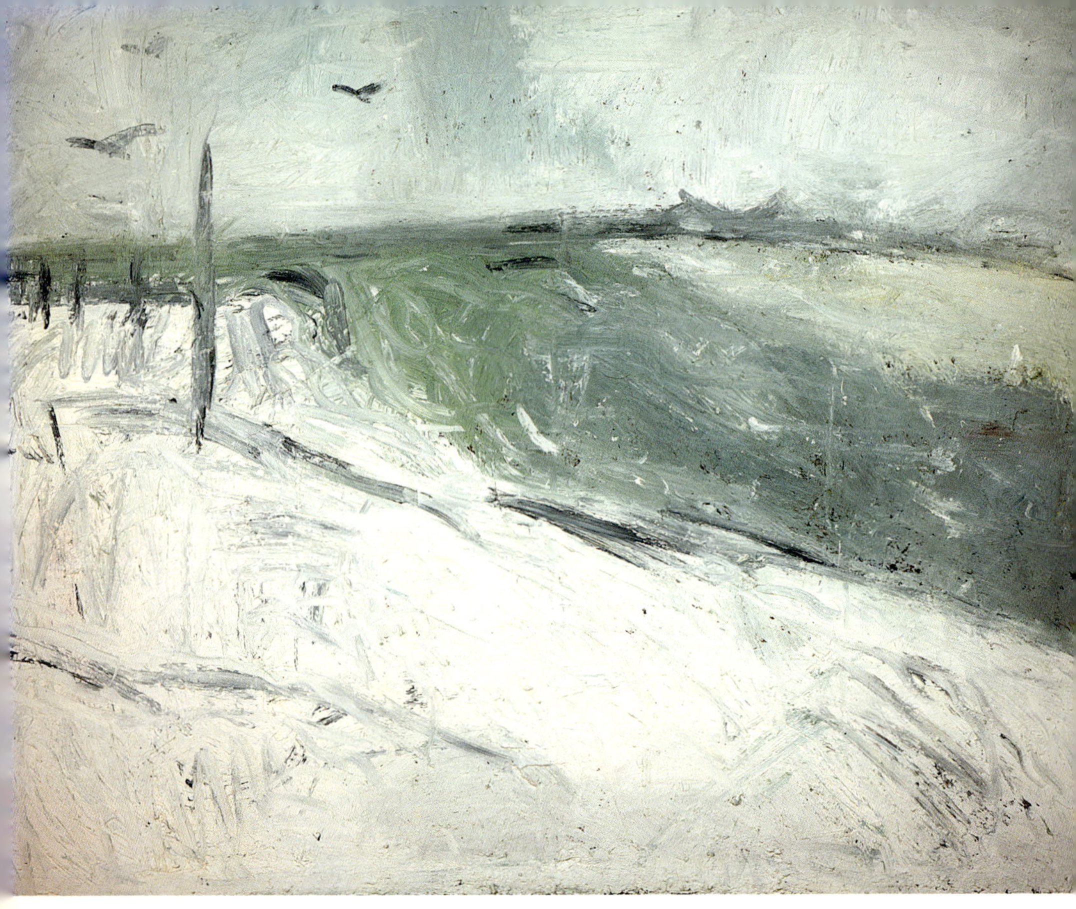

Richard Cook, Lelant, November, *1998. Oil on canvas, 153 x 200 cm*

power station across the bay to the east at Hayle (Nicholson and Stokes, having no head for heights, shouted directions from below). Hayle had once been a prosperous port and centre of copper production, but trade declined and the harbour silted up. The

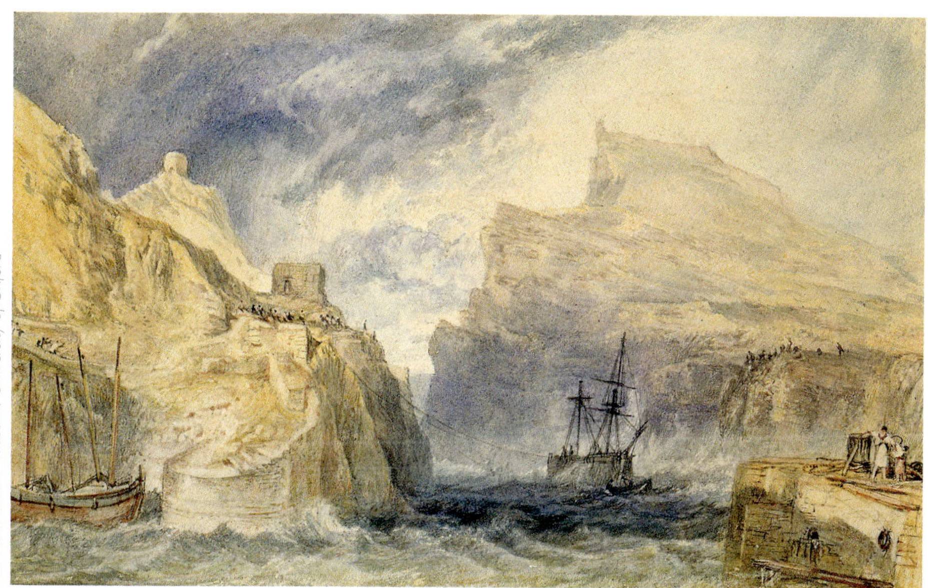

J.M.W. Turner, Boscastle Cornwall, *c.1824. Watercolour, pencil, pen and ink on paper, 14.2 x 23.1 cm*

wide sand dunes and beaches that run the length of St Ives Bay divide here, where the Hayle River empties into the sea, creating fast, treacherous currents. St Ives, a couple of miles across the water, takes on the appearance of inaccessible, dreamlike distance. The strange quiet and openness of this spot comes through in Richard Cook's paintings, which carry an undertow of danger in their tension between calm, pale colour and turbulent brushwork. 'Landscape,' Cook says, 'is a place without destiny... In order to have a feel for landscape you have to lose your feeling of place' (page 108). By contrast, John Miller, whose former house overlooks the river and the beach beside the estuary, painted this same location as though forever transfigured in the deepest, peaceful blues of high summer.

Beyond stands Godrevy lighthouse on its humpbacked rock, a chalky exclamation mark punctuating the easternmost tip of St Ives Bay. Alfred Wallis brought it into his paintings again and again. It's there, too, on the tiles Bernard Leach made for the flat top of Wallis's grave in St Ives's Barnoon Cemetery, and in innumerable other paintings of this coast. Godrevy is, in fact, the last point on the return trip up the north coast of Cornwall to have been so intensively gazed at and interpreted by artists. The cliffs and coves extend onwards from here towards St Agnes Head, where Lanyon took off on his glider flights, to Newquay, Padstow, Tintagel and up to the Devon border near Bude, but art somehow didn't become entangled in the life of these places to anything like the extent it did further west.

In Turner's watercolour of the fishing port of Boscastle near Tintagel, a ship is being winched through choppy water into the narrow harbour, its sails furled (page 109). Turner magnified the height of the cliffs to either side, so that the scene resembles an episode from the Odyssey rather than a working day by a Cornish quayside. Yet hazard and drama, as he'd seen so clearly at Land's End, are never far from the surface along this coast: Boscastle became briefly world famous in August 2004 when a flash flood destroyed much of the village centre, sweeping buildings and vehicles out to sea. Not far inland, up the Valency Valley (whose steep course accelerated the floodwater), is the church of St Juliot, to which the young architectural draughtsman Thomas Hardy was dispatched in March 1870 to assess the crumbling building for restoration. It was at the rectory next door that he met his future wife, Emma. In his late poems of loss and recollection, Hardy imaginatively retraced his steps along the Cornish cliffs. Among all his intense personal associations with 'that wild weird western shore', it was its astonishingly changeable visual splendour – its colour and movement, 'the opal and the sapphire of that wandering western sea' – that held his mind's eye.

Index of Artists

Page numbers in red denote reproductions of works.

Public Collections

The Leach Pottery, Higher Stennack, St Ives TR 26 2HE
Tel: 01736 799703
www.leachpottery.com

Newlyn Art Gallery, New Road, Newlyn TR18 5PZ
Tel: 01736 363715
www.newlynartgallery.co.uk

Penlee House Gallery & Museum, Morrab Road, Penzance TR18 4HE
Tel: 01736 363625
www.penleehouse.org.uk

Plymouth City Museum & Art Gallery, Drake Circus, Plymouth PL4 8AJ
Tel: 01752 304774
www.plymouth.gov.uk/museumpcmag.htm

Royal Cornwall Museum, River Street, Truro TR1 2SJ
Tel: 01872 272205
www.royalcornwallmuseum.org.uk

Tate St Ives, Porthmeor Beach, St Ives TR26 1TG
Tel: 01736 796226
www.tate.org.uk/stives